FACE T

BY ARRANGEMENT WITH THE BRITISH BROADCASTING CORPORATION

FACE TO FACE

Edited and introduced by HUGH BURNETT

Portraits by FELIKS TOPOLSKI

Stein and Day/Publishers/New York

CONTENTS

First published in the United States of America by Stein and Day, 1965
Published in England in 1964 by Jonathan Cape
Copyright © 1964 by Hugh Burnett and Feliks Topolski
Library of Congress Catalog Card No. 65-17933
All rights reserved
Printed in the United States of America

INTRODUCTION
Hugh Burnett

When I was a boy I once cycled to Ayot St Lawrence to interview Bernard Shaw for my school magazine. It was a warm summer's afternoon and Shaw's Corner dozed in the sun. On the way to the front door I passed a window. Inside sat Shaw, his feet up, in an armchair, closely scrutinizing the current copy of *Lilliput*.

Shaw gave me the interview. He pretended to be gruff and commented on the reckless quality of the questions. He got rid of me by saying that he had work to do, which I had interrupted.

When I got home I checked on that magazine. Far from working, Shaw had been studying a set of portraits of himself drawn by Feliks Topolski. That was my first glimpse of the face behind the public face and it looked interesting. In a way that was when FACE TO FACE first began. Since then I have seen many public men and many public faces. Without exception the private faces have proved to be very much more interesting than the public faces. And it was the elusive private face we were trying to capture in FACE TO FACE.

The television programme started life as a series of B.B.C. short-wave radio broadcasts to listeners in the Far East. To show aspects of British life and character, a number of differing and interesting people were interviewed in their homes. In these recordings they answered many personal questions concerning their backgrounds and beliefs, and far from shrinking from the probe they seemed to enjoy the experience. Lord Birkett, Bertrand Russell, Augustus John, Henry Moore and Evelyn Waugh were among them. Indeed, the visit to Mr Waugh at his home in Gloucestershire was followed by the account of Gilbert Pinfold's preoccupations with questioning voices and sounds in the air, which Mr Waugh later identified with himself.

The patterns of questioning in these programmes provided a blue-print for the television series. And television brought a new, vital dimension—the opportunity to study in close detail faces and reactions of people under pressure. This close-up television situation was matched with a third vital ingredient, the searching comments in line by Feliks Topolski, the portraits which opened and closed the programmes.

Lord Birkett was the first guest on FACE TO FACE.

It was a live transmission, as were most FACE TO FACE broadcasts, and much of the character and success of the whole new series depended on his candour and co-operation. We plotted together as we had often done in the past. He enjoyed broadcasting and he liked the challenge of attempting something new. He promised to be frank, and, in line with his candour, the cameras pushed in close, to carve his wise old head against the black velours, the back hairs rising characteristically away from his scalp in a gentle arc.

After the transmission was over, we were all sitting together discussing the way things had gone when the door burst open and in came Gilbert Harding, puffing and blowing. He had rushed out from his flat in London to offer congratulations at first hand. And as he did so the telephones rang again and again as viewers packed the switchboards.

From then on FACE TO FACE gathered momentum. The pattern was varied to bring a wide variety of people and professions to the screen. Sometimes visitors were caught as they passed through London—Adlai Stevenson and King Hussein were invited in this way. Sometimes people were flown in from abroad. Martin Luther King came in from Alabama, Simone Signoret from Paris. Sometimes cameras were taken abroad when people were out of reach. Professor Jung was filmed at his lakeside home outside Zürich. Jomo Kenyatta was finally persuaded to come before the cameras in Nairobi. Normally each programme was preceded by a portrait sitting at Feliks Topolski's studio, but sometimes this procedure had to be varied. Kenyatta was drawn under conditions of great difficulty as the filming took place, Feliks, with pad, moving silently through the grass to get new vantage points. Jung was the only one who refused to be drawn, which is why no portrait of him appears in this book.

FACE TO FACE was fortunate in having a brilliant interviewer. And the programme had a new formula for his role. Usually a television interviewer, in programme terms, is psychologically and visually equal to the man he is addressing. The FACE TO FACE back-to-camera technique gave a new interpretation to this function. While the interviewer was the spokesman for the viewer, the viewer could indulge his curiosity in

THE INTERVIEWER

John Freeman

uninterrupted scrutiny of the guest. This alignment helped everybody. It gave the speaker a reason for being on the screen. It freed the interviewer from unnecessary attention and scrutiny. And it brought the viewing public face to face with distinguished men and women under circumstances of particular interest and candour.

One of the most important functions of television is the honest display of human beings to one another. When this happens, it becomes possible to judge whether the standards and beliefs being held up for approval are really as valid and generally supported as we are led to believe. Social progress is slowed by isolation, and one of the great advantages of good television is that people are exposed to wide varieties of views and attitudes quite different from their own. FACE TO FACE kept on demonstrating that people were not as they were supposed to be—that a public face had been obscuring them from view.

One incident pinpoints the purpose of these programmes. Standing in his garden beside the lake at Zürich, Jung was watching us trying to film the floating captions in the water. This was his favourite place by the jetty, where he came in the mornings to feed the moorhens that lived in the rushes. He leaned on his stick, grinning and puffing his pipe as the pieces of paper sank or floated out of reach.

'Professor Jung,' I said, with a straight face, 'I would like to start this film with a shot of you coming out of the lake from your morning swim.'

'Ah, yes,' said Jung, pulling himself erect, 'emerging from the unconscious!'

Here are some fragments of FACE TO FACE. They are set out in a manner akin to the mood the programme tried to convey. This is not intended to be printed television. These are some of the highlights, some of the glimpses of other people's lives, taken from their eye-levels, with their prejudices and opinions. This book is a permanent record of a few of the infinite and marvellous moments of human experience and belief, as seen by a rare and remarkable group of men and women. I hope they have done themselves justice.

What one is trying to do is to relax a man enough so that he will show himself as he really is.

The notion that television interviewers have great power, I think, is much to underrate the intelligence of the viewers.

Any effective interview to be done toughly must be done either from an opposite point of view or, at any rate, from a carefully thought out position which tests the validity of the other man's position as ruthlessly as can be.

THE INTERVIEWER
John Freeman

John Freeman

People appear on this programme by their own choice; nobody has ever been subjected to any sort of improper pressure; the names of those who, being invited, have preferred the haven of discreet obscurity have never been divulged—nor yet those of that more sanguine company who hopefully press their claims to public exposure.

Is it desirable to remove the wrappings from our public figures? I think it is. I think that, in an age which is perhaps contributing more to the art of packaging than to any of the deeper seated virtues, responsible public opinion is strengthened by the ability to meet public figures without their masks.

Face to Face has set out, not only by its methods of questioning, but also by the unwinking scrutiny of its cameras, to enable the viewer in his home to meet the famous with an immediacy and intimacy possible in no other medium and to pass his own judgments on them.

Occasionally the process of unwrapping will reveal a private reality shocking to those who value cosiness above all else in their viewing; but that risk is inseparable from the process itself.

I think without exception I always tried to ask questions in a courteous manner.

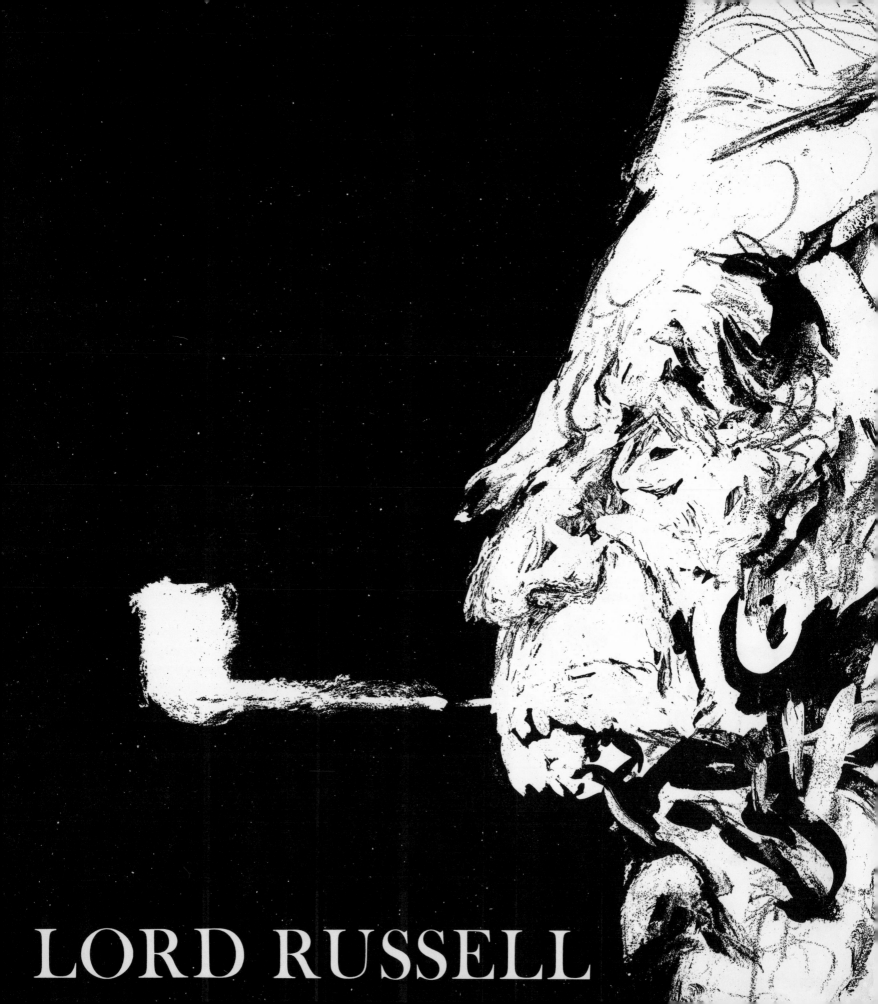

LORD RUSSELL

By the death of the third Earl Russell, or Bertrand Russell as he preferred to call himself, at the age of ninety, a link with a very distant past is severed. His grandfather, Lord John Russell, the Victorian Prime Minister, visited Napoleon in Elba. His maternal grandmother was a friend of the Young Pretender's widow. In his youth he did work of importance in mathematical logic but his eccentric attitude during the First World War revealed a lack of balanced judgment which increasingly infected his later writings.

Perhaps this is attributable, at least in part, to the fact that he did not enjoy the advantages of a public school education but was taught at home by tutors until the age of eighteen, when he entered Trinity College, Cambridge.

In the Second World War he took no public part, having escaped to a neutral country just before its outbreak. In private conversation he was wont to say that homicidal lunatics were well employed in killing each other but that sensible men would keep out of their way while they were doing it.

Fortunately, this outlook, which is reminiscent of Bentham, has become rare in this age which recognizes that heroism has a value independent of its utility. True, much of what was once the civilized world lies in ruins, but no right-thinking person can admit that those who died for the right in the great struggle have died in vain.

His life, for all its waywardness, had a certain anachronistic consistency, reminiscent of that of the aristocratic rebels of the early nineteenth century. His principles were curious; but such as they were, they governed his actions. In private life he showed none of the acerbity which marred his writing, but was a genial conversationalist, not devoid of human sympathy. He had many friends but had survived almost all of them. Nevertheless, to those who remained, he appeared in extreme old age full of enjoyment, no doubt owing in large measure to his invariable health, for politically during his last years he was as isolated as Milton after the Restoration. He was the last survivor of a dead epoch. " [1]

That I wrote in 1937, a year before the Second World War began, as a prophecy of what I thought The Times would say about me when I died. I observe that the date I attributed to my death is 1962, which is coming ominously near and begins to cause me some alarm.

[1] Published in *Unpopular Essays* by Simon and Schuster. Inc.

My mother died when I was two and my father when I was three. I remember nothing of my mother. I remember my father once giving me a leaflet printed in red letters, and the red letters pleased me.

My grandfather was already an invalid. He could only get about in a bath chair. He died when I was six. My grandmother survived for a long time, till after I was married, but she lived in semi-retirement. We saw a lot of distinguished people and especially literary people.

My grandfather was twice Prime Minister. My father was in Parliament for a very brief period. He lost his seat in Parliament in 1868 for advocating birth control and on that sort of subject my grandmother would not have agreed with him at all. In purely political issues she shared most of his views.

I have a great many memories of Mr Gladstone. He had an eye that could quell anybody. People who didn't know him can't quite understand his political importance. It depended on his hawk's eye. My most painful recollection of him is when I was seventeen and very, very shy, and he came to stay with my people and I was the only male in the family and after the ladies had retired after dinner I was left *tete-a-tete* with Mr Gladstone; and he didn't do anything to alleviate my shyness. He made only one remark. He said, 'This is very good port they've given me but why have they given it me in a claret glass?' And I didn't know the answer.

My grandfather, Stanley, whom I don't remember because he died before I was born, wouldn't allow his daughters to read Thackeray because Thackeray was so true to life and he took pains that as many as possible of them should marry into the peerage.

My grandfather's heir, Lord Stanley, who succeeded my grandfather, he had a most disastrous career. He married a Spanish lady of unknown origin and he got to hate her bitterly. After he and she were both dead it turned out, what he'd never known, that he was not really married to her because she had a husband living!

I wasn't a sceptic when I was very young. I was very deeply religious and lost my conventional beliefs slowly and painfully—very slowly. I remember—this is another very early memory that I have—that when I was four years old they'd just been telling me the story of Little Red Riding Hood and I dreamt that I had been eaten by a wolf and to my great surprise I was in the wolf's stomach and not in heaven.

I suppose I stopped saying my prayers when I was about twelve or thirteen. I was made to say them at first but I went on after I'd stopped being made to.

They told me when I was an infant that angels watched round my bed while I slept and I'd seen pictures of angels and I thought I should very much like to see one. But I supposed that the moment I opened my eyes they fled away. So I thought well the next time I wake up I won't open my eyes and they won't know. And I did so and I made a grab, thinking I should catch an angel. But I didn't!

I had one brother who was seven years older than me and I had very little to do with him. And otherwise I didn't have very much to do with other children. So it was a solitary childhood. But it wasn't unhappy.

They asked me one day what was my favourite hymn and I chose 'Weary of Earth and Laden with my Sin'. I was then six years old.

I don't think I had any guilt about sex. I don't think I had much occasion to.

I was never fond of the classics. Mathematics was what I liked. My first lesson in mathematics I had from my brother, who started me on Euclid and I thought it the most lovely stuff I'd ever seen in my life. I didn't know there was anything so nice in the world. I remember it very well. But I remember that it was a disappointment because he said, 'Now we start with axioms.' And I said, 'What are they?' And he said, 'Oh, they're things you've got to admit although we can't prove them.' So I said, 'Why should I admit them if you can't prove them?' And he said, 'Well, if you won't, we can't go on,' and I wanted to see how it went on, so I admitted them *pro tem*.

Mathematics gave me sheer pleasure, the sort that people get from music or from poetry. It just delighted me. And then, apart from that, I thought that mathematics was the key to understanding the universe and I found all sorts of everyday things explained by means of mathematics. I remember I had a new tutor once who didn't know how much I knew, and I spun a penny and he said, 'Do you know why that penny spins?' And I said, 'Yes, because I make a couple with my fingers.' And he said, 'What do you know about couples?' I said, 'Oh, I know all about couples!'

Until I was about forty, I got the sort of satisfaction that Plato says you can get out of mathematics. It was an eternal world, it was a timeless world. It was a world where there was a possibility of a certain kind of perfection and I certainly got something analagous to religious satisfaction out of it.

The First War made me think that it just won't do to live in an ivory tower. This world is too bad and we must notice it.

I thought, as a politician, and I still think that it would have been very much better for the world if Britain had remained neutral and the Germans had won a quick victory. We should not have had either the Nazis or the Commun-

ists if that had happened, because they were both products of the First World War. The war would have been brief. There would have been nothing like so much destruction. I still think that that is valid. That is speaking as a politician. Speaking as a human being, I used to have occasion to go to Waterloo, and there I would see troop trains going off, filled with young men who were almost sure to be slaughtered and I couldn't bear it. It was too horrible.

I wasn't actually pelted with rotten eggs but I had an almost worse experience. I was at a meeting of pacifists at the Celtic Brotherhood Church and it was stormed by a mixture of colonial troops and drunken viragoes. The drunken viragoes came in bearing boards full of rusty nails with which they clamped everybody on the head, and the colonial soldiers looked on and applauded them and the police looked on and did nothing and women had all their clothes torn off their backs, were badly mauled and so forth and so on. The viragoes

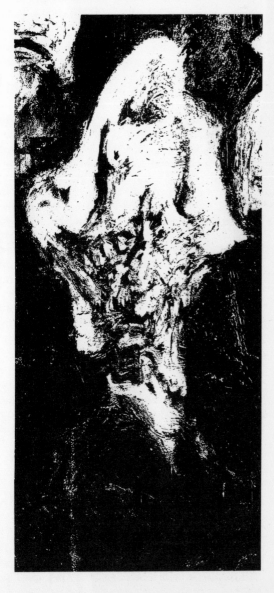

with rusty nails were just about to attack me, and I didn't quite know what one did about this, when somebody went up to the police and said, 'Look, you really ought to stop these women, you know. He's a distinguished writer.' 'Oh,' said the police. 'Yes, he's a well-known philosopher.' 'Oh?' said the police. 'He's the brother of an earl!' And then the police rushed and saved me.

I was convicted for writing an article which they said was 'intended and likely to cause bad relations between England and the United States'. I had pointed out how United States' troops were used as strike breakers. It was thought I oughtn't to have done that. The magistrate said this was the most despicable crime. He sentenced me to six months and originally it was six months as an ordinary criminal and then on appeal it was altered to six months in the First Division possibly because my brother knew everybody concerned and when the Home Secretary wasn't being very obliging my brother went to see him. 'He was my fag at Winchester; he'll do it.' So he did.

There was a whole rabble in New York of un-educated Irish people and they had completely, absolutely ignorant views. There was a woman who was intending to send her daughter to the College of the City of New York, where her daughter was not going to study mathematical logic which was the subject I was going to teach. Nevertheless, this woman professed to be afraid that I should rape her daughter, or corrupt her in some way, by my mere presence in other classrooms in the same university. And on that ground she brought an action that I should be deprived of my position and she accused me of being lewd, lecherous, lascivious, obscene and aphrodisiac. And all of these charges were upheld by the judge in court and the judge said that he would therefore annul this appointment. It was proved that I had said that an infant under six months old if seen touching his parts should not be slapped. That was the chief evidence.

I was completely ostracized. No newspaper would print a word I wrote. No magazine would print a word. No hall would allow me to lecture in it. I was cut off from all my means of livelihood and I couldn't get any money out of England at that time because of currency regulations and so I was expecting to starve. I had three children whom I was educating, two of them at the university and one younger, and I expected we should all suffer very badly. And we should have done but for a certain man—I'll call Dr Barnes—who came to my rescue and gave me a job.

I had a letter from an Anglican bishop not long ago in which he said that all my opinions on everything were inspired by sexual lust. And that the opinions I have expressed on this subject were among the causes of the Second World War.

I was left a certain amount of money. When I came of age I had capital that brought me in about six hundred a year and then I became a Socialist and I came to the conclusion that I ought not to live on inherited money and I got rid of my capital gradually to various causes which I thought important; and since then I have lived entirely on my earnings.

Fanaticism is the danger of the world. It always has been and has done untold harm. I think fanaticism is the gravest danger there is. I might almost say that I was fanatical against fanaticism.

I thought all along that nuclear war in which both sides have nuclear weapons would be an utter and absolute disaster. Now, there was a time just after the last war when the Americans had a monopoly of nuclear weapons and offered to internationalize nuclear weapons by the Baruch proposal. I thought this an extremely generous proposal on their part, one which it would be very desirable that the world should accept. And I thought—not that I advocated a nuclear war—but I did think that great pressure should be put upon Russia to accept the Baruch proposal and I did think that if they continued to refuse, it might be necessary actually to go to war. At that time nuclear weapons existed only on one side and therefore the odds were the Russians would have given way. I thought they would, and I think still that that could have prevented the existence of two equal powers with these means of destruction, which is what is causing the terrible disaster now. I should have been prepared to use nuclear weapons on the Russians. They were not, of course, nearly as bad as these modern weapons are. They hadn't yet got the H-bomb. They'd only got the A-bomb and that's bad enough, goodness knows. But it isn't anything like the H-bomb. I thought then and hoped that the Russians would give way. But, of course, you can't threaten unless you are prepared to have your bluff called.

I smoke a pipe all day long except when I am eating or sleeping. I took to it some seventy years ago so it doesn't seem to have had a very great effect, so far. In fact, you know, on one occasion it saved my life. I was in an aeroplane and a man was getting a seat for me, and I said, 'Get me a seat in the smoking part because if I can't smoke I shall die.' And sure enough there was an accident, a bad accident, and all the people in the non-smoking part of the plane were drowned and the people in the smoking part jumped into the Norwegian fjord where we'd landed and were saved. So that I owe my life to smoking. I was rung up by a journalist in Copenhagen and he said, 'What did you think while you were swimming in the fjord?' So I said, 'I thought the water was cold.' And he said, 'Did you not think about mysticism and logic?' And I said, 'No,' and rang off.

I should like to say two things; one intellectual and one moral. The intellectual thing I should want to say to them is this. When you are studying any matter or considering any philosophy ask yourself only what are the facts and what is the truth that the facts bear out. Never let yourself be diverted either by what you would wish to believe or by what you think would have beneficent social effects if it were believed, but look only and surely at what are the facts. That is the intellectual thing that I should wish to say.

The moral thing I should wish to say to them is very simple. I should say: love is wise, hatred is foolish. In this world, which is getting more and more closely interconnected we have to learn to tolerate each other. We have to learn to put up with the fact that some people say things that we don't like. We can only live together in that way and if we are to live together and not die together, we must learn the kind of charity and the kind of tolerance which is absolutely vital to the continuation of human life on this planet.

I wrote Churchill a very impudent letter. I wrote him another one, too, if it comes to that, but I wrote him one rather impudent letter about the miners, during the miners' strike of 1926. I said the government was trying to force them back to work by starvation, and that I wouldn't stand for it, and this was pretty good cheek, coming from a boy who'd just got into Parliament at the age of twenty-six. But instead of getting angry with me, he wrote a five-page letter in his own handwriting, and six weeks later asked me to become his parliamentary private secretary.

It all began to go wrong when I became a minister in his government. Churchill offered me the job of Under Secretary for Food, and then somebody told him that I was intriguing with Lloyd George—what about, or what I *could* intrigue about with Lloyd George, who was ten years older than him, I've never been able to discover. There was no intrigue of any sort or kind. I think it was because I was discovered lunching at my club one day with Mr Lloyd George at a moment when the political corridors were full of rumours, and it was a question whether he was going to join the government. Anyway, the fact remains that it was reported that I was intriguing with Lloyd George and there was no truth in it whatsoever. But then I did another thing, which was fantastic on looking back on it. After Dunkirk I got rather worked up about the condition of the country, so I sat down one summer morning and I wrote to the Prime Minister a letter telling him how I thought the war should be conducted. Now, if I'd written a humble little letter saying that I thought the public should be encouraged to eat more herrings, that would have been very appropriate from the Under Minister of Food. But I told him all about how to run the strategy of this country, what to do with France, where to put the fleet, where to put the troops and, finally, what to do in the event of the invasion of this country. And I received a letter, summoning me to the Cabinet Room, where he was alone. Instead of, as I confidently expected, my ideas being sympathetically considered—and you can remember the burden he was bearing at that time—I had that letter scorched, sentence by sentence, and when I finally tottered out from Downing Street, I suddenly realized what fearful impudence it had been; what a mistake I'd made. I managed to get back to the House of Commons, and then I did something that I've never done before or since in my life. I ordered a quadruple whisky. It was very necessary, and indeed it hardly made any improvement.

Not long after the war I found myself at Boulogne with a motor car and two pounds, and I had a trip back in the ferry, and so I had to decide whether to have a little supper in Boulogne and sleep in the car or sleep in Boulogne and have no supper. And suddenly I thought, my goodness, I'll go to Le Touquet. And I went off to Le Touquet, and this is all true—nobody will believe it—but I went to the most expensive hotel and I ordered a most tremendous dinner and I went into the casino with my two pounds and there I found a gypsy sitting there, and the gypsy said, 'You follow my advice. You'll be absolutely O.K. but you've got to give me a lot of your winnings,' and I never took any other advice, and in two hours I'd turned my two pounds into four hundred and fifty pounds, so I was able to pay for my dinner!

I've tried to be constructive now and again. I've been a rebel in so far as I have been a rebel, first of all because I do care passionately, whatever people say to me or of me, about public affairs, and because I think so often these politicians make such a frightful mess of it. And then I naturally get rebellious. I have to be.

The tide of office missed me, and I think the probable reason is that I didn't want office *enough*. I wasn't prepared to sacrifice enough in order to get office. I hadn't got that *kind* of ambition. And when the Prime Minister saw me and made the suggestion that I should go to the House of Lords, he knew that, and I knew that, and I confess I jumped at it. I think it's a wonderful solution. I love it. I've now got a platform. I can say what I jolly well like. I think the standard of debating in the House of Lords since I've been there is considerably higher than that of the House of Commons.

LORD BOOTHBY

I was doing all I could to avoid violence, and in many cases I have denounced violence in my political meetings and otherwise. I did so but I think my denunciations were not given wide publicity because for one reason or another the authority—the government—wanted to paint me as black as they could. I don't know how much they could. I don't mean black by colour, but I mean painted black in character. And they tried to put all the evil thing on me, which was not, of course, true.

You see when a man is hungry and he sees somebody, his neighbour, going with a full belly, naturally he resents it, human nature being what it is. You can't blame the Kikuyu feeling that this land belonged to us and now here we are with nowhere to cultivate or to graze our cattle, sheep and goats. I think that is one of the reasons which made the relationships deteriorate. The Kikuyu could see, whenever they passed, this land which, a few years ago, had been theirs.

Missionary have done a lot of good work, because it was through missionary that many of the Kikuyu got their first education, and through the missionary institution many Kikuyu were able to learn how to read and write. Because the missionary wanted them to be able to read the Bible in their particular languages, and also the medical side of it the missionary did very well, and are still doing some good work. At the same time I think the missionaries, some, especially the old missionary, did not understand the value of the African custom, and many of them tried to stamp out some of the customs without knowing, or thinking, the part such customs play in the life of the Kikuyu. I think through that, or through interference with the people's custom, they upset the life of the people. But on the other hand they did very good work.

I'm a Christian. I believe in the teaching of Christ, the way He taught, and which I take it many so-called Christians do not follow. I've no quarrel with them—they can do what they like—but I believe in the teaching, the way Jesus taught. I follow that line, but I don't like denominational kind of business because sometimes this is also due to selfishness of human nature. That is a small section of people, or a small sect feel that their way of interpreting the Bible is the best. I don't follow that, I follow the teaching of the Bible, and I think it helps me in many ways.

I don't play a second fiddle, I wouldn't do that. I feel I am controlling the party, and I'm capable of doing it.

We don't want to rob anybody of his property. We are not concerned with robbing people of their property. But what we want to get is power, that is, the government. We want to rule our country, and those people who want to stay in this country can do so, providing that they accept it.

We want help from those who can give us help. We want help from all quarters, administratively, or economically and otherwise. What we don't want is those, what we call in Swahili, Bwana Kubwa. We don't want Bwana Kubwa—we want friends, those who can work under an African government. We want them. But what we don't want is masters. Those who want to be masters must find somewhere else, because what we want is friends to help us. Those who can help us, but masters—no. We have no place for them.

KENYATTA

IN PRISON *I was just a mere convict, known by number, not by name. I was told that that was one of the punishments to deny me all the privileges that I had before. I was treated just like a common prisoner.*

I like to be tidy. I like to be tidy; I like to be colourful. I hate things to be drab. I can't stand being drab. I mean, one doesn't want to be flamboyant, and of course it's difficult, I suppose, to draw the line between colourfulness on one side and flamboyance on the other. I hope I don't drop down on the side of flamboyance, but I'd rather be flamboyant than drab.

I first wore an orchid—I don't know—it started, I suppose, in the nineteen twenties, because my father had a collection of orchids which he had at Haywards Heath. He had an orchid grower there, and then from time to time there was a plethora of orchids—it's always feast or famine in those things. The orchids came on all at once and no one knew what to do with the orchids so little Nubar had an orchid—Nubar's myself, you see—had an orchid sort of thrown in, and I thought they rather suited—I don't know about my style of beauty—I wouldn't like to say!—and I've worn them ever since. Now, actually, I've got a few plants of my own. In theory I always like to say I have an orchid from my plants every day of the year but that's not strictly true. I mean, let's be quite frank about it, I mean, I've got a very good orchid grower who helps me out.

I suppose I'm extravagant. I know when I was small I always used to live on next year's income. But I mean, as an economist, I think it's a great thing to do, because in an inflationary cycle you're spending good money and paying back in bad.

My father was a man of a great foresight, great energy, and great willpower, and he had the foresight as far back as eighteen ninety or so, when oil was merely a thing that one used for kerosene lamps,

to see that it would have a great future. And he travelled in the Caucasus before the Baku oilfields were discovered, and he wrote quite a learned treatise on that at the age of twenty or thereabouts, which was published in a very highbrow French review. He thought that oil would be a thing of the future, and he went into it chiefly from the negotiating point of view, the diplomatic point of view. Not so much the commercial —he didn't buy and sell oil—but from the combination of interests, politically and commercially. The origin of his five per cent—the famous five per cent—was that he obtained concessions from the Sultan of Turkey about—oh, I don't know—1900 or so, and there were various oil groups fighting to get concessions. I mean, with respect, his greatness was that he saw if all these people competed against each other no one would get anywhere. His idea was get them all together. At one moment he had forty per cent of it. He let the other people in and it came down to twenty-five per cent. He ended up as five per cent, but his idea was always it's much better to have a small slice of a big cake than a large slice of a small cake.

He had a five per cent share. He took his chances with the others. He put up his cash, and he took the risks. If the thing had gone wrong, well, he'd have lost. Until the ship came home there was quite a lot of cash had to go in there.

He had a very good system with check, recheck and counter-check. If one technician said one thing and he thought, well, that seems funny to me, then he'd ask another technician. The same way with lawyers. He had one lawyer who'd say one thing. He said, well, that looks all right, or looks rather phoney, so he'd ask somebody

else. After all, the problems of business are really like the problems of life. They are really problems of common sense.

He hated publicity. He hated the press. He hated publicity. He'd run a mile to avoid a photographer or to avoid a press interview. He was always a very modest man. He liked to live his life to himself. Several times as the story goes— but not as the story goes—the story *is* so—I think it was nineteen eleven when the House of Lords threw out Lloyd George's budget, and Asquith had threatened to recommend to the King the creation of a certain number of peers, and people were going around looking for prospective candidates for peerages, and he was approached, indirectly, if you like, and he wouldn't have it. Of course, we used to live—I was fourteen in those days, my sister was ten—we used to live in Hyde Park Gardens. My sister who was quite a wag even then—two children talking together—said to me, 'Oh, what fun it will be if Papa gets a peerage! He'll be Lord Bayswater, and we'll be the Honourable Lancaster Gates!' I don't want to talk without the book or anything, but I think if you read the memoirs of the time there was a standard fee. Before the last act came in, there was an honours act or something, just about that time. There was a standard tariff—I think it was twenty thousand for a baronetcy and a hundred for a peerage—I don't know. I mean, it's not fair to . . . But, he wouldn't pay anything.

He was an Armenian and it had always been a tradition in our family that we should always marry Armenians. I'd been brought up in England and there weren't so many Armenians about. So the chief objection to my first

marriage was that the lady was not an Armenian and was not of our religion. He had visions of, you see, another Armenian girl who he would have handpicked, and then we'd have carried on the dynasty or traditions, if you like. That's what he had in mind and that upset him.

I was very fond of my father. I was terrified of him. I respected and admired him no end. But, of course, I was terrified of him.

He was a man who had a very strong will, a will of his own, and I suppose the real trouble was that we were perhaps too much alike. You see, probably, I was spoilt—I mean, I must have been an odious little boy—but after that, sometimes, from time to time, I felt— one always does when one is twenty-five—one feels one's grown up, one's capable of running one's own life. And I decided I wanted to marry—that was for the first time—which he objected to. There was another thing. He was very keen on knowing everything which goes on. He had a great attention to detail. For instance, right up to his death, the menus of the servants at the house in Paris, the daily menus, were always sent to him so he should know exactly what the servants had so they should be well fed. And then he was looking through the petty cash book apparently at the office one day and he found, 'Lunch, Mr Nubar'. I think it was a pound or fifteen shillings, whatever it was. And he was very, very annoyed. He hauled me over the coals about that. He said, 'What's that? You've got a very large allowance. You can buy what you like; you go and charge your lunch to the office.' Well, I was very annoyed about that. It was very silly, of course. I had had the chicken sent in because I'd had a lot of work to do

that day and I knew I wouldn't have been able to go out to lunch and one thing led to another. And then we had a row. We had a lawsuit—a very silly lawsuit. The chicken cost—Father very kindly paid all the costs—it cost thirty thousand pounds—one of the most expensive chickens there was!

As far as I'm concerned, I was left very comfortably off—I still am very comfortably off. I'm not worth a billion dollars. I think Mr Paul Getty says, 'A billion dollars is not what it used to be'—well, it was. I'm not worth a billion dollars or anything like that, but I mean I've got enough to keep body and soul together comfortably.

There's no question of saying that the Gulbenkian Foundation was set up without my knowledge, or

without my consent even—not that I had any consent to give. But my father felt, and I agreed with him, that when one talks of *very* large sums—I mean five or six million pounds a year—it's quite wrong for any one individual to have the handling of that. But the executors of the present Foundation are not the people running it that my father wanted. Secondly, they aren't running it as he *would* have wanted.

I'd advise a rich man to teach his children to be independent, and to stand on their own legs, and look after them while they're young. Start them off on the right road, and then let them make their own way. They'll enjoy much more a hundred pounds they'll have earned themselves than a thousand pounds that Papa will have given them.

Dame Edith Sitwell

I can't wear fashionable clothes. I'm a throw-back to remote ancestors of mine, and I really would look so extraordinary if I wore coats and skirts. I would be followed for miles and people would doubt the existence of the Almighty●I'm descended from the most queer and remote sources. On one side, my maternal grandmother is descended straight from the Red Rose Plantagenets, the Dukes of Beaufort—my grandmother was the daughter of the Duke of Beaufort of her time. On another side, I'm descended from an errand boy who walked barefoot from Leeds to London and built up a large fortune. I'm extremely proud of his having walked barefoot from Leeds. His niece was the woman who was known as the wicked Lady Cunningham, who was my great, great grandmother. She was so wicked she stopped the flogging in women's prisons and was going to stop the flogging in men's prisons in the army and navy, but George IV died, so this wicked woman was left to her own devices, having only prevented the flogging in women's prisons●I live with my eldest brother, Osbert, at Renishaw, in Derbyshire.

and for part of the year I go with him to his Italian home, Castello di Montegufoni, an extremely romantic house outside Florence. The tower and the great castle wall were built by the Dukes of Athens, the Acciaiuolis—in eleven hundred and something—when the Dukes of Athens were thrown out of Athens by the Turks, and they came to Montegufoni. They were not always very hospitable. If people came out from Florence whom they didn't want to see, they just threw boiling oil on them from the castle walls.

My personal hobbies are reading, listening to music, and silence.

I have been, in my life, very much influenced by the works of Mr Stravinsky—more for excitement than for being soothed.

I sit and wait for inspiration.

I have an *extremely* small income—smaller than anyone could think—and I have always earned my own living. I've been excessively poor. I'm always supposed to be extremely rich.

My father was rather an odd old gentleman, and during the First War I had to take a job which brought me in twenty-five shillings a week, and two shillings war bonus. I did that partly out of patriotism, but partly because I was too poor to live without it.

I don't think I'm forbidding excepting when I absolutely refuse to be taught my job by people who know nothing about it. I have devoted my whole life to writing poetry, which is to me a form of religion, and I'm not going to be taught by people who don't know anything about it. I think it's very impertinent. I mean, I don't teach plumbers how to plumb.

My father and mother married without knowing anything about life at all. They were quite young. My mother was seventeen, and poor thing, she didn't know anything about life. She was just made to *marry* my father, and they just didn't understand the first thing about each other. My mother was very beautiful. My father was a wild eccentric. When I was a child I was fond of him, only between the ages of thirteen and seventeen, because he was then kind to me. Then he suddenly turned round on me. I've never found out why.

I was a changeling, you see. When I was born my mother would have liked to have turned me into a doll. It was a great disappointment to them that I was not a boy. If I'd been Chinese I should have been exposed on the mountains with my feet bound.

I don't think my mother bothered about my appearance. My father loathed it. He liked people covered with curls and quite frankly, rather common. You see, he'd married a lady, and it hadn't gone very well, so he didn't want any more ladies about.

They resorted to everything which could possibly humiliate or hurt me.

When I was a small child, my dear old nurse was wonderful. And then there was the fascinating Henry who came of a long line of whalers, who was first of all footman and then butler. He came when I was two years old. He used to button up my shoes, when I was put into a perambulator, and he would always, in after life, come to me and say to me, 'Look out, miss. You'd better get out of the back door because her ladyship's coming for you.'

Until my brothers were born, my only companions were birds. I loved the wild birds. But my pet birds—there was a peacock, and he and I loved each other very much, and I was four years old and he had a kind of feeling for time. He would fly up to the leads outside my mother's bedroom when I went to say good morning to her. And when he saw me he would give a harsh shriek, and he would then wait for me until I came out again, when he would give another scream and fly down into the garden and wait for me. We would then walk round and round the garden, as you might say, arm in arm, excepting he hadn't any arms; I would have my arm round his neck. I was four years old, and I was asked why I loved him so and I said, 'Because he's proud and has a crown, and is beautiful.' And then my father got him a wife, with his usual tactlessness, after which he never looked at me again, and my heart was broken.

I ran away from home when I was five. I couldn't put on my boots, unfortunately, and so was captured at the end of the street and brought back by a policeman, whom I hit as hard as I could, but I was restored.

My father lived in the thirteenth century where a groat was quite a lot.

I have tried in every way to avoid personal publicity, since I was of a certain age. I mean, when I was young I didn't care so much. If people make fools of themselves, all right they make fools of themselves. Since I was very young, I have avoided it.

When I die I will be able to say that I think that I've given more devotion, and had more devotion, than most people I know.

'. . . But the great sins and fires break out of me
Like the terrible leaves from the bough in the violent
    spring . . .
I am a walking fire, I am all leaves—'

The great fire, I suppose, is a humble but unworthy love of God, and certainly a great love of humanity. And to be an artist is a terribly painful thing. I mean, the great leaves break out of me—you see, one has a perpetual resurrection in one's life, as the art returns to one, after long deadness. You see. And of course the fire's always fighting the sins, and—well, there one is.

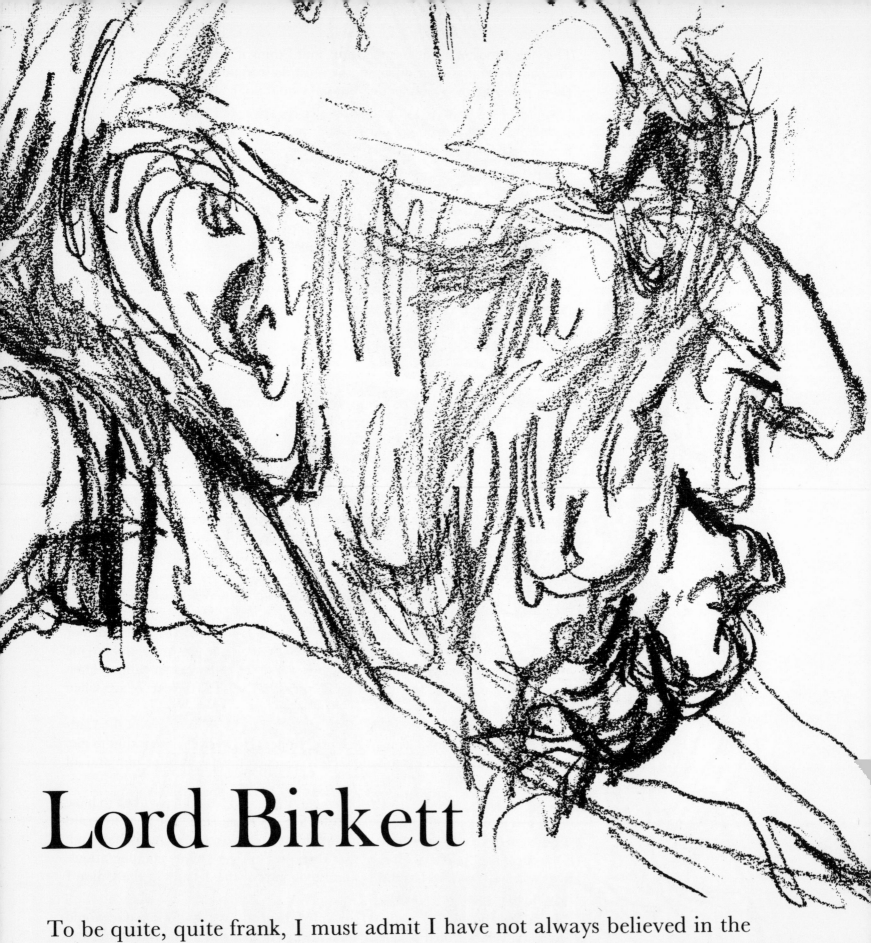

Lord Birkett

To be quite, quite frank, I must admit I have not always believed in the innocence of my clients . . .

The view I took of the advocate's duty, and I think it's the right one, is that he's there to present one side only, and he must do it to the very best of his ability. He must do for the man what he himself would do, had he the ability to do it.

I would be against tricks of all kinds. If I were asked, 'Do you regard it as your duty to do everything within your *power*, within the *rules*, to get a man acquitted?' I would say yes.

An advocate is not allowed to defend a person he knows to be guilty. You may *think* that he is guilty, and of course it's really quite impossible for any man of sense to have a brief to defend some man, and read all about the facts without coming to some conclusion in his mind, but what he *thinks* is quite irrelevant. He's not the judge. He must present his side of the case, the other side must present theirs and let the judge decide.

I have never known a case where a man was wrongly hanged. I could recall one case during the war where a young man was *convicted* who ought not to have been convicted, at least, in my opinion, but it's so rare that that's about the only case that stands out in my mind. But he was not hanged. He went to penal servitude.

I found a very great fascination in winning twelve people to my point of view. There is a very great attraction and fascination in the exercise of persuasive speech. It's quite impossible to persuade a jury by talking nonsense, and the thing that you say must at least have the appearance of sound sense; otherwise it's no good. And when you're presenting that to the jury, you must certainly give the impression that you are sincere.

None of my family had ever had anything to do with the law. I'd never been in a police court. I'd never been in an assize court, I knew nothing about the law when I decided to go to the Bar, and I think—I've often wondered myself—I think the reason was that it offered the best opportunity for using such facility or gift as I had for public speech.

My father had a drapery business in a little town in the North of England and it was his dearest ambition that I should follow him in that business, and as I cared for my father very much I was very anxious to do what he wished. For some years I was in the business with him, but then it became quite plain to me that I really couldn't continue. I began to yearn for rather wider things. Then I went to Cambridge, and ultimately to the Bar. I was thirty years of age when I was called to the Bar.

I earned money by becoming a private secretary. I went to one of the Cadburys in Birmingham—George Cadbury, Junior. He was very, very kind to me, and I was with him as his private secretary, made his speeches for him and all sorts of things.

I went to the grammar school at Barrow in Furness. I would have liked to have gone to a public school. I'm not sure that it was a wise regret, but I've often said I'd like to have made a century for Harrow at Lord's or something of that kind. On reflection I'm not at all sure that there weren't very many compensations. By the time I went to Cambridge and took part in the debates at the Union I was a fairly practised speaker.

My father and mother were Wesleyan Methodists, and I suppose one would say very, very devoted people. I shall always be grateful for my home life and for the chapel life to which they led me. My knowledge of the Authorized

Version of the Bible and the hymns of Wesley and Watts are certainly some of my very greatest possessions and at the most formative period of my life I shall never cease to be grateful for the training that I had in religious things. I do not have these beliefs today. As one grows older one rather grows out of certain ideas, and although I have my own very strong views about the conduct of life and the qualities which are necessary for the conduct of life, the great doctrinal things rather perplex me and trouble me. I would call myself a Christian, but, of course, you've got to define your terms. I believe in what are called the Christian qualities. Sometimes I would like to say that I call myself a Christian-Agnostic. I don't know whether that term is permissible.

My life at the Bar certainly was the happiest period of my life. It stands out in my mind as compared with being a judge, or a Lord Justice, or anything else. It was a really happy time, though every moment of one's day, and almost night, was spent in that work.

I was earning a lot of money and we had opportunity of good nurses, and household staff, and things of that kind, but I'm bound to say that so far as the children were concerned, I didn't do very much in the way of personal supervision.

I earned many thousands—perhaps it would be enough for me to say that when I became a judge, at five thousand a year, it was a terrible financial sacrifice.

My clerk's reports of a salary in the region of thirty thousand a year would not be untrue. Anything that he said wouldn't be untrue. That would be an average figure, sometimes below it, sometimes above it.

One of the advantages in my day was that you could save a little. I paid very large sums in taxation. But I was always a thrifty man in that sense, largely because of my upbringing, I suppose, and I did save.

I wasn't really drawn to the judicial office. I loved the Bar so much. It wasn't the money, but I loved the life of the Bar, and I think the life of a judge (and I've proved it since) is a bit remote and a little lonely. You're necessarily withdrawn from the ordinary life of the Bar.

Sometimes, as a judge, when I listen to cases being conducted, I felt how much I would like to be down there doing it.

Quite contrary to my expectation, I had always rather dreaded the time when I was to pass my first death sentence. But when the actual moment came, I did it without the slightest trace of emotion. It was a case during the war where a young sailor had betrayed the position of a convoy to the Germans. The Germans attacked and sank the convoy, and the charge I think was under the treachery act. When the moment came for me to sentence him to death, I did it without emotion at all. It's very curious how impartial you become when you sit in the seat of justice. I won't say you become inhuman. That would be quite wrong. You must keep your human sympathies, and your human faculties all alert. But I think you get a detached, dispassionate outlook upon things which permits you to do your duty.

At the Nuremburg trial, Goering, for a very long time, simply dominated the court. He was a man of very great personality, and when he came to give evidence in the witness box he did very well indeed. I never did come to like Goering, largely because I knew his history, and I knew the kind of man he was. The kind of man for whom I felt a little sympathy was a man like Speer who was only brought in by Hitler towards the end.

There was a little difficulty at first in working with the Russian judges. I sat next to General Nikitchenko throughout the hearings and we became the greatest possible friends. It is much to my regret that when we left Nuremburg and he promised to keep in touch with me, I never did hear from him, though I inquired. I wrote to him and my wife sent him and the other judge a wonderful album of photographs covering the whole time we were there, and fountain pens and all sorts of things. Never any acknowledgment. At first the Russian judges were very recalcitrant. If a proposal was raised by one of the German counsel in favour of the defence the Russian judges were against it, without any argument at all. One had to try and persuade them to come to one's point of view. But it was very, very difficult. But ultimately we worked together.

The only question I think that can really be asked about Nuremburg is, was it a fair trial? I think it was. The Charter of 1945 which governed all the activities of the tribunal certainly set down the law as it existed. It was not a creation of law, it was international law as it existed. It said that superior orders shall not be a defence, but it may be a mitigation.

The real disappointment of my life was that, being a Liberal, the Liberal Party, when I was ready to take part in elections, was on the decline, and therefore I could never be a law officer of the Crown, because you must be in Parliament and your party must be in power. That's really one of the disappointments, because when one goes to the Bar one rather hopes that politics and the Bar together will lead one a good long way.

At the time I was in the House of Commons I was far too busy to attend to it. That was the trouble. I never got down there until about five o'clock in the evening, and then I had to get up all the briefs for next day. It was that kind of life. I think that the very busy man really cannot combine the two.

ROY THOMSON

I think I've got ninety-five newspapers. It was ninety-three. Now it's ninety-five. And I think it's seventy-two magazines.

I'm not a selling man—I very rarely sell a newspaper—I'm a buying man.

I like the newspaper business. It's a business—a profitable business when it's well operated. It's a business that has a lot of prestige, and I think it's a much better business to be in, for instance, than the grocery business, or making steel, or doing some other line of activity, which no doubt I would have been in, had I not been in the newspaper business.

If I start to give orders to my papers, even in something that I'm sure is correct, then where do I draw the line? The next thing I'm interfering in politics, I'm interfering in other aspects of it. I cannot run a large number of newspapers on any other basis than complete editorial delegation, and I practise it religiously. Many of my papers say things that I completely disagree with. I do nothing about this. It's not so much morally, or ethically, but, I mean, I think their judgment is bad in many instances. I often gnash my teeth when I read a leading article in one of our papers that I know has been written with insufficient knowledge of the subject. I have more knowledge of the subject and I'm sure they're wrong. But, after all, again I cannot interfere with them on that. They're doing the best they can as they see things in that community and I leave them alone to do it.

I'm for the Common Market.

I'm for capital punishment.

I am for the rearming of Germany.

I am against nationalization. I'm a regular Tory.

I'm a Protestant, loosely speaking. I would go to any Protestant church, but I don't often go. I think I have the usual religious beliefs. I believe implicity in the Golden Rule. In this day and age I'm afraid we're all sinners, and I don't claim to be any better. But I hope I'm not any worse than anybody else. I do honestly try to live by the Golden Rule, "Do unto others as you would have them do unto you.' Perhaps I don't always succeed. But I believe in that implicitly.

I read a lot—mostly thrillers.

Mostly I like the light television programmes—the comics—and I like programmes such as this—discussion programmes—and, of course, always the news.

I don't think I'd buy the *Daily Herald*. I mean, you don't want to buy a headache and that's really a pretty big headache.

STIRL

I am frightened of death. It's something every driver should be frightened of. If I go too fast I certainly am frightened and very conscious of what I've done. You get a sort of tingling of the hands and a feeling as though you've just eaten a lot of porridge which goes right down, you know, to your feet! That's the sort of sensation I get. But I wouldn't ponder on the thought.

I think fear is really lack of understanding of what is happening.

In Syracuse there was one corner which I had never taken quite flat out, at this time about a hundred and fifty miles an hour, and I was always just easing off. Well, in a racing car there is a big difference on your time—when I say a big difference, a tenth—between easing off and absolutely flat on the floor. But there's also psychologically a very big difference—you feel you're dead safe lifting off, but if you keep your foot down you're near in trouble. And I came into this corner and the only way I could bring myself to taking it flat out was by looking down at my instruments, not watching the road you know, setting the car up and then looking up when it was too late to lift off—and that is the time when I have to screw up my courage. And also going on to a banked track like Monza, where you've got to get the car up at about eighty degrees. This also frightens me because of the extra possibilities of mechanical failure.

Death is something which frightens me and thinking of it isn't going to make it less likely to happen, therefore I don't think about it.

At Monza, my steering sheered at a hundred and sixty five on this banked track and my arms just shot round like this and the thing was out of control and I had virtually no brakes and I remember going up, hitting the top of the wall, and closing my eyes, forcing back on the steering wheel with my feet, and then there was a whole hooha—I don't know exactly what happened because I had my eyes closed—and the car came to a standstill. I jumped out and there was dust

NG MOSS

and everything, and I remember thinking, well, if this is hell, you know, it's not very hot, or if it's heaven, why is it so dusty, you know, and I was absolutely convinced that I was a goner.

I had a tyre burst at a hundred and twenty and I lost control and shot across the road because I was taking a corner when my outside front tyre burst and there was a big wood there and I shot across and I thought, well, this is my lot. I'm going to go straight into the woods at a hundred

and twenty. I managed somehow to regain control in time, or the car came back—anyway, something happened and it was all right and I felt frightened while it was happening but immediately after I didn't get the feeling of fear because I had something else to think about. The tyre was burst, my second position was lost, I had to get back to the pits and so on.

It is a calculated risk but there are unfortunate things which you can't calculate for which are mechanical failures and oil on the track. I am not normally afraid of killing myself. I'm frightened of being killed by something over which I have no control.

I wouldn't like to dive off a very high board but I'm not frightened of heights, no. I'm not frightened of aeroplanes. I don't think I'm frightened of any of the normal things.

I trust myself but I must admit that if I think about it now I trust that God is with me and helping me. I'm religious inasmuch as I believe that there's a God. I'm not religious inasmuch as I don't believe in going to church. I had too much of it thrust down my throat when I was at school, when I was forced to go into church when I didn't fully understand it. I wasn't, I suppose, interested. I'd go in there and be looking around and not really concerned about what was going on. I really and truly don't feel that I'm any better for going and standing up and singing hymns or praying with a lot of other people than I am on my own.

We have in motor racing practically all superstitions, which I follow—you know—you wouldn't light three cigarettes with one match and wouldn't walk under a ladder. There are superstitions which go too far, such as when you see a blood-wagon—an ambulance—some people cross their fingers and count three dogs! Well, this would mean I'd have to drive all the way round the race with my fingers crossed, and it's not very practical! So I feel I have, with reservations, all the superstitions.

Originally I was supposed to be a dentist and I'm not really that brainy. I couldn't get through my exams, so we had to throw that over. Then my father and I discussed it and we thought, well, the hotel business was an interesting one, so I started as a trainee in that.

The professional driver has to go fast whether he's got the stomach ache or not and if he gets into a car he's expected to go faster than any other amateur's gone in that car. Whether he

knows the car or whether he knows the circuit, doesn't really matter.

I have expensive tastes. I mean, there are quite a lot of things which I haven't got that I would like but I prefer it that way. I don't think I'd like to have everything I want. I find certain things, anyway, in life rather frustrating and I think that would increase the frustration. On the other hand if they're small things, then I can buy them if necessary.

I would retire if somebody passed me on a corner in a similar car. If I felt that somebody was going considerably faster than me and my car was right, then I would retire.

I like taking a pretty girl out, I like a luxurious flat as well. Funnily enough, cars don't worry me too much. I find it a little frustrating driving on the roads and a car to me is much more a means of conveyance. I like dancing and going out and generally doing something other than motor racing. I don't mean I don't enjoy motor racing. I do, but I also enjoy going in go-karts and water skiing and any type of sport.

When I started racing I was much more of a hermit. Until very recently I took it easy for quite a few days before the race. I didn't go out and so on, and what good did it do me? I didn't get the world championship or anything else. So I suddenly thought, well, let's live it up a bit, and now this year I have been. I've been dancing —not the night before the race but up until a couple of nights before—I've been out dancing and really swinging it and having a lot of fun, and it doesn't seem to have yet affected my driving and my personal, social life is very much more fun. So until I get some proof that it's not the thing, I suppose I'd like to continue doing it.

I don't take pills on principle. I don't go to sleep easily unless I go to bed late and therefore I do go to bed late. I find that if I go to bed at twelve I'd think until three o'clock. If I go to bed at two o'clock I've got a good chance of being asleep at two or two-thirty.

What does worry me is if I think that I've driven a bad race. That would really worry me, whether I won it or lost it doesn't really matter. It's annoying if you go out in a race—you know, you're leading or you're well positioned and then suddenly something breaks. This is annoying, it's frustrating, but it doesn't worry me. But if I went out into a race and I drove what I felt was a bad race and won it, this would worry me mentally far more.

Oo-o! I would try to stop any son of mine from being a racing driver. Racing has brought me my greatest happinesses I suppose, and quite a lot of unhappiness. I think I would try to stop him from being a racing driver because I'm inclined to be selfish. I think what my mother and father have to go through must be absolute hell. I really am very sorry that I can't find anything else that gives me what I want and yet is more unselfish towards them. I would try to stop him.

KING HUSSEIN

I was very, very fond of my grandfather, King Abdulla, and I used to stay with him, in office, practically the whole of every day, right from seven in the morning until the time when he retired, about ten-thirty at night. I only used to go to the house for very brief periods during the days, because I really was so—so happy—to have had a chance to spend some time with him. I really loved him in every way.

My mother always was a source of encouragement to me. I've tried to better myself in every way, and I think my mother had quite a bit to do with that. My grandfather on the other hand gave me his love and affection and really every day I spent with him was full of lessons in how to serve and how to be a leader. I think the impression that some people might have that my mother has influenced me in my work, is quite wrong. She has been always a friend and a source of encouragement to me, but whenever there were any decisions to be taken I've always tried to take them my own self.

I remember—I was about fifteen and a half—one day before that Friday in particular where the accident or incident took place in Jerusalem, I'd been up to the palace at Amman and my grandfather had said that he was going off to Jerusalem and that many people were not going with him who had various excuses, and would I like to come with him? I said immediately of course, and we departed the second day, Thursday, and we spent the night in Jerusalem. Friday we went to visit Nablus and on that morning my grandfather waited almost for half an hour, more than he should have, because he had given me the rank of an honorary captain and promised me to be his aide as well, and on that day I wasn't wearing military uniform. So he asked me to wear it and I couldn't find it, so that was a source of delay that morning. Then we went off to Nablus and West Jordan and came back to prayers. A few days earlier my grandfather had said something to the effect that he wished me to promise that I would be a servant of my people and would not let his work be lost. He had served them for thirty years in that country and he felt he might not be living very long. And I gave that promise, not knowing that not too long from it, an incident that I'll always remember in my life was to occur, and a great loss for me. We departed to the mosque, I remember, and there were rows of soldiers and troops lined up outside it, and it seemed to upset my grandfather quite a bit and he told them to go away because that was not a place where he liked to see people in uniforms. And they did. I was just about three paces behind him when we entered through the gate and suddenly I saw someone rush from behind a door to the right side with a revolver in his hand and before anyone could do anything, he fired a shot. My grandfather was hit and fell. It was a shock. I tried to rush for the man and he turned and fired. I received a bullet that ripped off a medal off my chest and then there was plenty of fire. He fell as well. I was beside my grandfather and with the aid of some—two people —who were present we carried him out, but unfortunately he had lost his life.

I wouldn't say I was completely a natural observer of the law at school but I didn't get in trouble very much.

At Sandhurst I changed from a normal young person to a man, or someone who understood a bit about responsibility. And both physically and mentally I went through a change in a comparatively short space of time.

I think I would send any sons of mine to school in England. Of course, if that ever did come about I would like to give my children what I did not have—a chance to receive in the way of education, to give them a period of studies and a period of growing up as they should normally do. I wouldn't like to force them to take any particular subjects; I'd like to leave it to them, to see what they're best inclined towards.

I have attempted, and have achieved, I believe, to remove many of the barriers that exist between the king and the people. I live with them. I spend most of my time with them, as one of them. I move freely about in the country, I spend quite a portion of my time studying their conditions, learning of their needs. A normal day in my life would be to begin my work around eight or just past eight, by either going to my office or to some section or part of the government to see how work is being done without that being announced, and in my work at the office I meet anyone who likes to come and see me no matter what walk of life he's in, to see what I can do to help them, and I spend in my office until two, or sometimes until four or five or six, then if I have any free time in the afternoon I either go flying with other pilots in the Royal Jordanian Air Force or go to visit some units, or go to a match of some nature somewhere, and spend most of the other time with my family. I spend in Jordan quite a bit of time in schools, and with our students that are a great hope for us for a better future, as well as with the armed forces, and other than that I live at a small house, a farmhouse, outside the capital, where I have to travel to Amman every day to work.

Once we had heavy snow in Jordan, and I took a jeep to the Jordan Valley. I took a jeep alone and went out and I was muffled up and I had on a head-dress, and suddenly I came to where there were on the road many cars that were stuck. I got out and tried to do something about it, but couldn't, so I started putting chains on the tyres. A soldier came and said, 'Do you think that this works?' I said there is a strong chance that it might. So he said, 'All right. I'll help you on one condition. If you can get through, will you kindly give me a lift? My village is further on.' So we worked, and he was instructing me every now and then to do something or another, and asking whether I knew how to drive this car very well, because if I didn't he did, and we worked quite happily, and then he got in and we moved on. We collected several others, and we were talking about all sorts of things. They were very happy because of the snow and the rain and how good that was, being basically farmers. And near the end of our journey they recognized me, and we kissed each other in the car and there was a big noise all over, and we continued, all of us helping the other cars that were stuck further on, until we reached an area where the snow had ceased. This type of thing happens quite often in my life and it gives me great pleasure and happiness.

I think I was probably about eleven when I first decided I wanted to be a sculptor. I remember quite clearly the instant. As a boy, at school, I liked the art lessons, I liked drawing. I used to get my elder brother to draw horses and other things for me from as early as I can remember. But the little incident that clinches the thing in my mind was that our parents used to send me and my younger sister to Sunday school on Sunday afternoons—to get rid of us I think mainly—and the Sunday school we went to was a Congregational chapel although we were Church of England. The superintendent every Sunday used to give a talk which always had some little moral. And one Sunday he told us about Michelangelo carving the head of an old faun in the streets—in his studio in the streets of Florence—and that a passer-by stood watching Michelangelo carving this head. And after watching two or three minutes he said to Michelangelo, 'But an old faun wouldn't have all its teeth in.' Michelangelo immediately, said the superintendent, took his chisel, knocked out two of the teeth, and there, he said, was a great man listening to the advice of other people even though he didn't know them. Now this story didn't stick in my mind for its moral but merely that there was someone—Michelangelo, a great sculptor. So instead of saying, as most boys might, that one wanted to be an engine-driver and so on, this pinpointed something in my mind and I knew from then onwards.

I remember a church about two miles from our home, a Gothic church, I think, between 1300 and 1400. I drew there as a little boy of nine or ten and always looked in there when I went to visit my aunt. That's about the earliest time I noticed sculpture around me.

My first serious lessons were when I went to grammar school, a co-educational grammar school. We had an art teacher, a Miss Gostick, half French, and she was wonderfully enthusiastic about the art lessons. Most of the boys and girls didn't seem to care about it, but I found that once I went to the grammar school I knew it was the one lesson of the week that I looked forward to. She was wonderfully helpful in asking me to tea every Sunday, and showed me copies of colour magazines and so on. I owe a great deal to her enthusiasm.

I was the seventh in the family. By the time I came along, one brother and two sisters had already become teachers, and this was the sort of path carved out for the rest of the family. So there was no question of me going down the pits. My father really was a remarkable man. Very ambitious for us children, and had taught himself, although I was told that he had no schooling and earned his living first of all at nine. In his youth I think there was very little public education, and by the time I remember him very clearly he could help me in my homework from the grammar school. He seemed to know the whole of his Shakespeare. He knew his Bible pretty thoroughly and he taught himself enough trigonometry, mathematics and so on to pass his exam as a manager for the coal-mine. So I think it was he who really helped the family. He was absolute boss, a

complete Victorian tyrant. I got on with him, but at the same time one had to keep away from his chair in the corner of the room, I remember. And homework, everything else, was done on the kitchen table after the meal was cleared away. His little corner was absolutely sacrosanct. Nobody was allowed to nudge him or bump him in any way whatever. I had a great respect for Father. I knew that his opinions had real foundation. For instance, when I came to want to be an artist, he said, 'First become qualified as a teacher like your brother and sisters have done and then change to art if you wish. Be sure that you have some living in your hand.' Well, this was very intelligent and very sensible, but by the time I got to that age I knew that I wasn't going to be a teacher, that I was going to study art.

There were two other boys at the school who ran neck and crop with me for favour with the art mistress, Miss Gostick, and we were given in turn the jobs of designing the school programme for the school concert, or the scenery, and there came a time, when the war began—I was still then only, what? fifteen—and it was decided to have a school Roll of Honour for the old students who were joining up. So I carved a scroll and a little scene on the top of it. This was the first real start of my proper carving career. I believe it's still there.

I got married when I was thirty. My wife was twenty. Straight from being a student I was put on to the staff of the Royal College of Art where I was a student for four years, and for that I think I got two hundred a year for two days a week. This one got married on, and before being married that two hundred was wealth. After we were married my wife had quite a need to watch and be careful with the money when we tried to entertain friends and so on, but we never seemed to go short of anything.

A sculptor is handicapped economically and young sculptors can't get their work cast into bronze. Bronze casting is a very expensive thing. In my case, I used to go round to the stone yards—the stone mason's—and take odd bits which had been knocked off other pieces. Random blocks, they're called. And these I'd store in my studio, and then as one got an idea that fitted one particular piece you could use it. I still have quite a lot of the same pieces that I gathered then, that didn't fit any idea, but in that way one got material cheaply.

The biggest stone I think that either I or anybody else have carved for a long time was the stone for the UNESCO sculpture. That cost over £3,000. That was a huge carving, much, much bigger than anything I've done or ever will do again. Marble can be anything from five or six pounds a cubic foot, and you soon mount up if you have two by four by four. It comes to quite a lot. I've known young sculptors who have stopped working because they can't afford the price of a bag of plaster, which is only fifteen shillings. And the transport is a problem. There's one figure of mine, a reclining stone figure which was the biggest I'd done up to then, which

almost made one bankrupt by having to send it out to exhibitions and pay for the transport and get it back. That was 1931. If one were sending this to, say, a London Group exhibition or to the Leicester Galleries or to some mixed exhibition, it might cost seven to ten pounds, and this would be a big amount out of one's income.

I hate commissions.

My works have been attacked and disfigured. I think this is just the work of silly hooligans—just silly people. Often it's better that no fuss should be made of it. And this is my line, that it's better to ignore those things. And even if something does happen and the Press rings me up, I pretend I don't know about it. That's the best way out of it.

My sculpture is based on an attempt to understand form. That is what a sculptor's life is built around— this use and understanding, appreciation. You've got to try to know what actual three-dimensional reality is like. And this isn't easy to know. This is something which you've got to do by steps and stages. One of the steps and stages in my attempt to understand what three-dimensional form was—that is, to try to know what the back of a thing is like when you're looking at the front of it—to try to know what, if I'm looking at you now, what your head—what shape it displaces in space—just what sort of angle it's at with your body. This is a chalk pebble for instance that I played about a bit on. When you see this side it makes you guess what the other side is like. Often the other side is different, but you do have this connection. And in my case the hole became as important as a shape, important as the actual material that surrounded it. The holes were an attempt to understand form.

The reclining figure is a subject which, for me, is unending. I think if I had five lifetimes I wouldn't exhaust the possibilities in this theme. It may be that it also connects the human figure with landscape more easily than a standing figure could, and landscape is one of my great obsessions, besides the human figure. I think it's a way of the two being amalgamated, but what it all means, I don't know really.

Some people have said why do I make the heads so unimportant. Actually, for me the head is the most important part of a piece of sculpture. It gives to the rest a scale, it gives to the rest a certain human poise, and meaning, and it's because I think that the head is so important that often I reduce it in size to make the rest more monumental. It's a thing that anyhow was done. The heads of Michelangelo's figures will sometimes go twelve times instead of the usual six and a half, which is the average. It is a recognized thing.

Sometimes I do things which are more—I don't know what word to use—probably more tender in their point of view, in their expression of the human figure. But other times, mostly, it's a power. It's what appealed to me as a young man about Mexican sculpture—its terrific strength, its terrific stony tension and vitality.

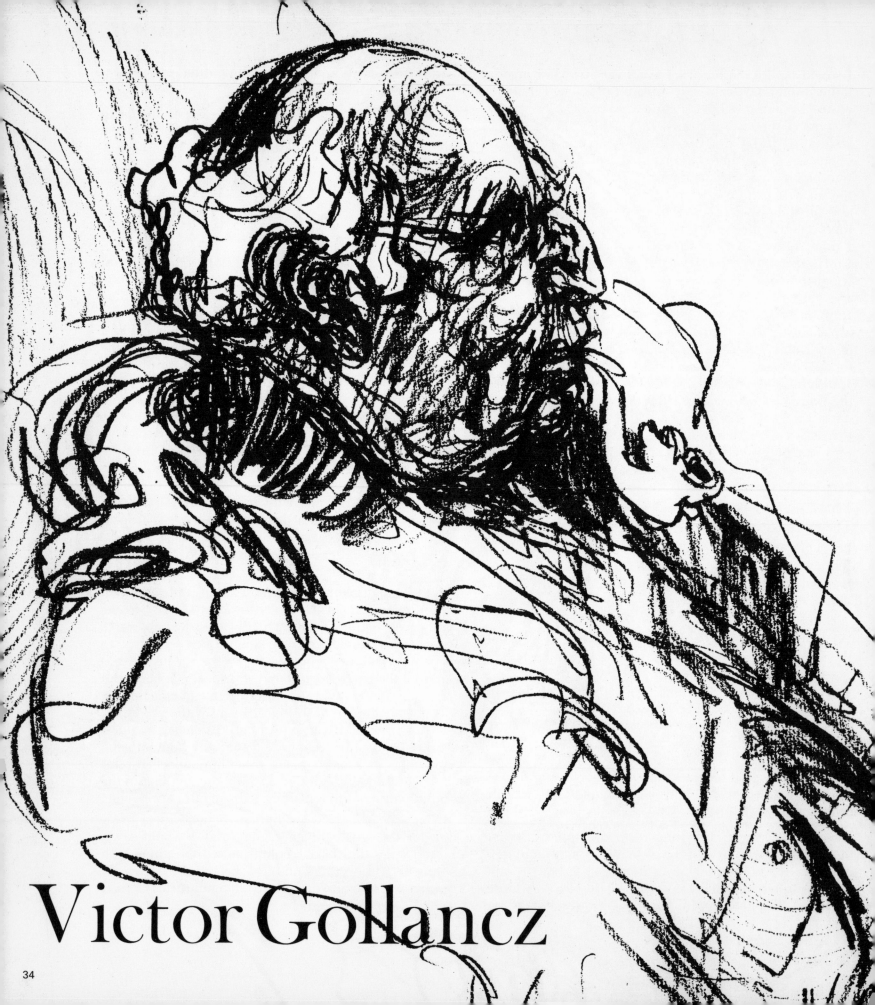

Victor Gollancz

I would say I am a bit of a Jew. A very bad Jew my late father would have said, but still a bit of a Jew. I think it's always been impossible to define what being a Jew means. For me, I suppose, it means that while a great deal in traditional Judaism is not only unsympathetic but even obnoxious to me, there's a certain way of looking at things that one derives from traditional Judaism, in particular the idea that there is no real division between the holy and the unholy, the sacred and the profane. All life, and indeed every 'lifeless' object, is in some sense sacred.

I don't practise any of the more obvious Jewish observances. I do practise certain things in the old traditional Judaism which I think very beautiful—such, for instance, as giving thanks every year on eating for the first time a fruit or vegetable you particularly like (with me it's asparagus). I had a little ceremony when I took possession of my country cottage, consecrating it and giving thanks for still being alive. When I enter a prison I say the old Jewish blessing, 'Blessed art Thou, O Lord, who loosenest the bound.' I have also on the doorpost of my London flat a thing called a *mezuza*—a little silver box with the first letter of the name of God showing through it—the idea being that every house is holy. I like preserving things of that sort, but I don't keep the Sabbath, and I haven't been in a synagogue since I married in 1919.

I have no feelings of any kind about race or nationality. The more variety, the more mixing, the better.

Forgiving your enemies was quite a possibility in remote Biblical times, and there's a lot about it in the Old Testament. But when Jesus told us to *love* our enemies, that was something completely new—it took morality into a totally new dimension. I believe it to be the secret of life.

When I started going to St Paul's at the age of about thirteen I used to travel by train from Westbourne Park Station to Hammersmith. The houses on the left down to Latymer Road were appalling—I mustn't be libellous, they mayn't be appalling now, but they were in those days—dreadful little houses, with all sorts of refuse, decaying fish-heads and such-like, in squalid back yards. And I used to think how awful it must be for people to live like that while I would be going home after school to lie on a sofa and eat raspberry jam sandwiches. That was the origin of my socialism.

By socialism I mean something quite different from what most people mean by it. I mean living with a community of goods, the kind of socialism that used to be true, and perhaps still is true, of life in the *kibbutzim* of Israel. Equal incomes? No. People with beastly jobs—scavengers and lavatory attendants and the like—should be paid a great deal more than anyone else.

I hate the business side of publishing—bargaining with authors, bargaining with agents, and all that. You have to do it, of course, but it's detestable.

My favourite pursuit is listening to music. I wouldn't call it a relaxation: it's an act of communion.

Corporal punishment I detested at school. I've always detested it. I've always thought it unmitigated beastliness.

We had on what used to be called, I don't know why, an 'occasional' table in our drawing-room in Elgin Avenue a huge quarto volume with an immensely thick blue binding, called *Sixty Years a Queen*—a record, I suppose, in celebration of the Diamond Jubilee. (My father was a great patriot, and thought very highly indeed of the Queen.) It was packed with illustrations printed on heavily coated 'art' paper, and one day I happened to open it at a place where there were two facing pages of pictures, reproductions, I imagine, of drawings. On one side was the Charge of the Light Brigade at Balaclava and on the other side the Charge of the Heavy Brigade, and in one or other of them a man on a horse was slashing down with a sword at another man's head. It produced in me a feeling of the most intense horror: I felt I was having my own head slashed off, and I thought, if this is war then war is an appalling evil and we must get rid of it. This was on my sixth or seventh birthday. I have longed to get rid of war ever since.

Far and away the cause I care most about is the abolition of capital punishment. However decayed I may become I shall never rest until we have finally abolished it. I agree with all the rational reasons against it, of course: to believe it's a uniquely effective deterrent, for instance, is against all the psychological and statistical evidence. But what really moves me is an entering into the feelings of the condemned man (or woman). I wait with him during those three weeks, I wait with him on that last night, I feel what he must be feeling; and that any human being should inflict such agony on any other human being seems to be so unspeakably evil that I would do anything in the world to get rid of this appalling stain on our national life.

I am an exceedingly weak human being with a great liking for the 'good things' of life, and I would say a hundred times that I have compromised too much with Mammon. If I were summoned before the Heavenly Tribunal and asked to defend myself against this charge, I think I'd prefer to be silent.

months later and the family, of course, spent almost the rest of its life in Southern Rhodesia.

My father made money all right but he lost it, and, of course, for the whole of my youth he was always very, very poor. I think he had bad luck but he was an adventurer and he was always chasing rainbows and always saw something better a little bit further on. I often wondered why we were always so poverty stricken, but I don't think my thinking ever went beyond that. I used to see other kids getting toys and enjoying many of the benefits that go with people who've got money but I don't think I was ever critical or resentful of it. I think my mother didn't like the events at times and it's not surprising because my father occasionally used to indulge in a bout of enjoying the wine of life. He used to cause some embarrassment to her.

I suffered with the stigma of being a Jew which one doesn't lightly shed in this world.

I became heavyweight champion of the Rhodesias by the time I was nineteen or twenty. I used to weigh about fifteen stone ten when I was in good condition. I've always been fat. I was fat as a kid. I weighed two hundred and eighty when I was about fifteen, what I weigh today. That was one of the factors that made me want to fight as well. I used to hate being called Fatty.

I learnt my lesson very quickly that the crowd support you when you win and if you lose you're in the dressing-room on your own. The sooner you learn that in this vale of tears the better for you.

My father ran what I think is almost giving it a status that perhaps it didn't enjoy—a doss house—he used to provide rooms in Salisbury. But I wandered off—I was about fourteen or fifteen then—around the mining camps and I worked in stores, butchers, I assisted a baker, I worked as a barman, and I wandered round doing anything and, of course, I got the feeling that I'd like something a little bit more permanent and something that would give one a bit more money. The railways—being keen on locomotives as most kids were—appealed to me. I applied for a job as a fireman and got it. I weighed two hundred and eighty pounds when I took it and then the first twelve months I lost eighty pounds, so it'll give you an idea it was fairly hard work.

At school I think I passed into standard five and that was as far as I got. I plugged standard four. I think I started work when I was fourteen, the year I turned fourteen. In certain circumstances, those standards wouldn't give me a vote in the Federation, but fortunately there are several qualifications; either financial or educational. I qualify under the financial.

In those days I was in favour of keeping the unions white. I think most white men were. That's a hard fact.

I know the African fairly well, you know. Of course, it's not easy for Prime Ministers to keep as close as it was for me as a youth with friends, but I have, if you don't mind me being perfectly blunt, swum bare-arsed with many piccaninnies in my poorer days, and I got to know them fairly well. I think I know the Africans and my own personal relationships with them are fairly good.

My father was an American citizen actually when he arrived in Africa and he, of course, had migrated from Europe. He originally came from somewhere near Vilna in Russian Poland. He migrated after the Franco-Prussian war of '71 to the States and spent some ten years there, heard about the diamonds that were being picked up in the streets of Kimberley, and decided that he would set sail for Africa. He arrived in Africa at the end of 1880 and didn't go in for diamonds. He bought ostrich feathers and made quite a lot of money. He was a wanderer, met my mother, who was South African Dutch, and married her. She was a girl of seventeen; he was a man of thirty-seven or closer forty possibly. He had a very large family—I'm the thirteenth of a family of fourteen. He was quite a wanderer and trekked all round Africa, and eventually walked up to the Rhodesias, walked up to Bulawayo, which was the centre then of European civilization as one might call it in Southern Rhodesia, about 1895, and of course did what most people did in those days, looked for gold and traded. My mother, of course, came up with five small children then in an ox wagon a few

SIR ROY WELENSKY

CECIL BEATON

There are many months in which I forget about photography entirely. I do that on purpose because I don't want to get stale at it. I've never had a studio, for instance, for the very reason that I don't want to have the responsibility to feel that I've got to clock in and take so many pictures each month. I want to try and remain an amateur at it, in order that I have the amateur's freshness and spontaneity.

I think I'm after expressing my instinct. I think I want to be creative, and I think I want to do something that I know is going to get somewhere towards my goal. And that goal doesn't really have anything to do with other people. If there is acclaim, I don't listen to it very much—I'm too busy getting on with the next job. I only wish that I did have a little more satisfaction in the things that I do.

I try to develop my intellect, but I know that it's really through my eyes that I work.

I had an idyllically happy childhood.

There are certain things one likes about people. One can dislike a person for their smell. I didn't dislike my father for his smell, but the world of the cricket pavilion and the 'Pink 'Un' and his rather hearty friends that he brought back to dinner on Saturday night, meant nothing to me. The sort of laughter in the billiard room was a world that I knew nothing of, and had a slight antipathy to.

I found school appalling—such a waste of time. I had my share of rooted, I was cold, I was hungry. It was during the First World War, and there was very little in the way of rations. I remember after a bit I got papillomas on my feet which were very painful, sort of corns produced by under-nourishment. And I just felt to begin with that I didn't like that sort of herding together. I hated the stink of a swimming bath in the morning. And it took some time to find one or two congenial friends, or people who I realized were hating it as much as I did.

I don't think money gave me much trouble at Harrow. I used to try and sort of slip chits with the housemaster for rather grander pyjamas than was supposed to be on the curriculum, and I used to go to the tuckshop and do pretty well there. I wasn't really hard up.

At Cambridge, new doors were opening to me. This was something that I'd never known before, and I was thrilled by the fact that certain people would give up their life to aestheticism. I thought it was lots of fun—I think I dressed in rather peculiar garb.

This hat I wear because I think it has a certain Edwardian bravura. I think its proportions in some way compensate for the deficiencies in my general geometry. And also it hides the fact that I'm going bald. I don't like to exhibit myself quite bald, you know.

Evelyn Waugh is my enemy. We dislike one another intensely. He thinks I'm a nasty piece of goods, and oh brother! do I feel the same way about him! My friends? Cyril

39

Connolly was at my first school, and, well, I suppose there were many at Harrow and Cambridge. Connolly hasn't influenced me, but I always respected his intelligence. Other influences, I think, have been the Sitwells, by remote control—Diaghilev enormously—Aldous Huxley. In his own way, I think, Cocteau—certainly Berard.

My father thought photography was a pretty rum affair. He felt he'd given me a good expensive education, and the only thing that I could come up with, having ruined his account books in his office for about three months, was that I should take a small house in St James's Square and take photographs on one floor, and design sets and costumes for plays on another. And I don't know what on the third. He thought it sounded very vague, and it was a bit of a shock, I mean, twenty-five years ago, maybe it's forty-five years ago, I don't know, photographers weren't thought of as being particularly eminent. He didn't think that I was going to be able to get to the top of the ladder in that way. . . . He helped me up to a point, but I think he was pretty exasperated really. My mother was sorry about the whole situation, but she was rather ineffectual, I'm afraid. She couldn't do much herself, and she didn't want to get unduly worried.

Success came quite by a fluke, and very unexpectedly. I took these photographs that were considered very revolutionary, and fantastic, and I had an exhibition of them. From the moment the show was on they just clicked because they were newspaper copy. There hadn't been photographs of what is known as celebrities—photographed in that particular way.

I wasn't very interested in the sitters.

I used to retouch very much more then than I do now. It was part of a feeling of the time. I mean I created a fantasy. I created a sort of dream world, and in that dream world you didn't want to see crow's feet, and veins in the neck. A few were rather appalled at the idea of being put under a Victorian glass dome, or reflected in the lid of a piano. But I really wanted to please myself, rather than them.

I think I prefer photographing women, but men are a cinch. One has to have a more lenient approach to women, and to combine the verisimilitudes and the sort of honesty of the attack, and at the same time be slightly kind. I think that makes the job a little more difficult. If it were a question of painting then one would put in the warts, but the camera has a very definite way of exaggerating the deficiencies. I don't approve of retouching, but if you see a perfectly straightforward photograph of a perfectly young and beautiful woman, there are certain things that are objectionable and have to be done away with. It's a sort of politesse.

I'm still looking for the end of the rainbow.

I'm always having to do things which are too difficult for me and I think that that is the thing that keeps me going. I think that I'm not an intellectual at all, but I feel that I need the company of intellectuals, so that something may brush off on me, from them. I want to do unpleasant things, because I feel that it's good for my character. I'm a terrific disciplinarian. I mean—again my father comes into this—although I loathe it, I very often, suffering from the cold as I do, have a cold shower each morning. I think one of the reasons why I'm here on television is that it's a challenge. It would be very easy to say—no, I shall just stay at home. But, all the time I'm trying to do things in my own way that I feel in some way help a bit. I haven't been able to ride a bike. I went into a holly bush after about the fourth attempt, and I thought, well, perhaps it's easier to walk. Occasionally I fight, but I'm perfectly willing to take on any job that I think may help make me a little better as a human being.

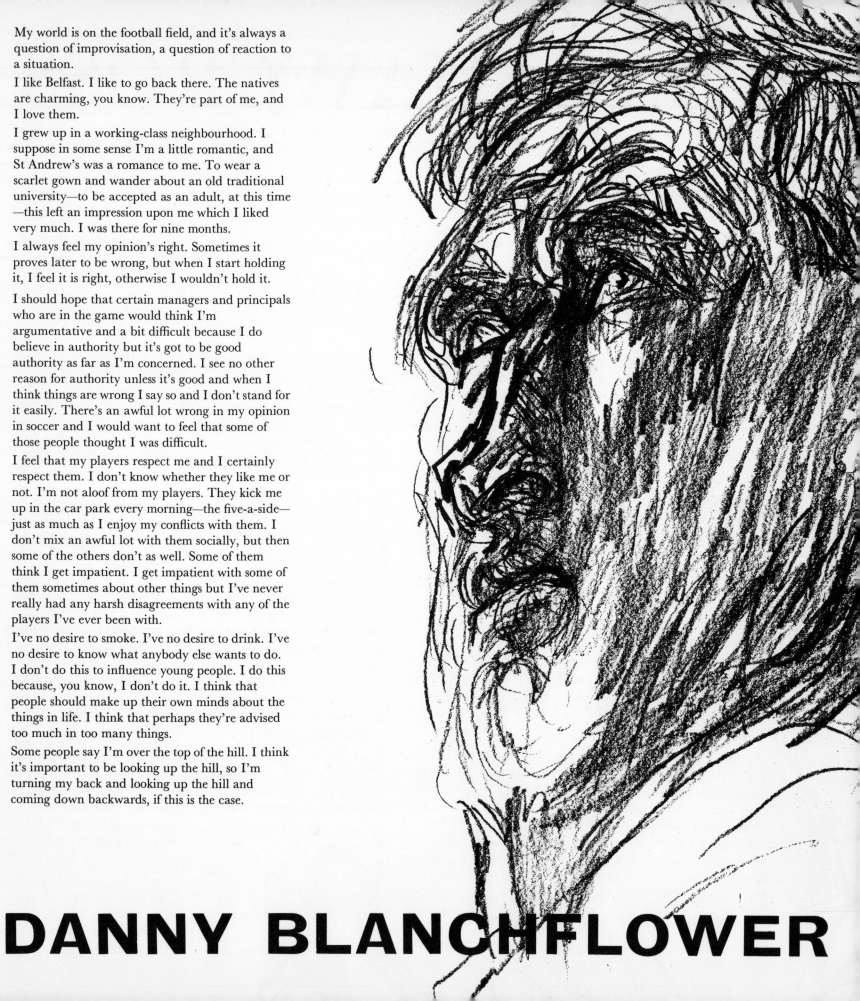

My world is on the football field, and it's always a question of improvisation, a question of reaction to a situation.

I like Belfast. I like to go back there. The natives are charming, you know. They're part of me, and I love them.

I grew up in a working-class neighbourhood. I suppose in some sense I'm a little romantic, and St Andrew's was a romance to me. To wear a scarlet gown and wander about an old traditional university—to be accepted as an adult, at this time —this left an impression upon me which I liked very much. I was there for nine months.

I always feel my opinion's right. Sometimes it proves later to be wrong, but when I start holding it, I feel it is right, otherwise I wouldn't hold it.

I should hope that certain managers and principals who are in the game would think I'm argumentative and a bit difficult because I do believe in authority but it's got to be good authority as far as I'm concerned. I see no other reason for authority unless it's good and when I think things are wrong I say so and I don't stand for it easily. There's an awful lot wrong in my opinion in soccer and I would want to feel that some of those people thought I was difficult.

I feel that my players respect me and I certainly respect them. I don't know whether they like me or not. I'm not aloof from my players. They kick me up in the car park every morning—the five-a-side— just as much as I enjoy my conflicts with them. I don't mix an awful lot with them socially, but then some of the others don't as well. Some of them think I get impatient. I get impatient with some of them sometimes about other things but I've never really had any harsh disagreements with any of the players I've ever been with.

I've no desire to smoke. I've no desire to drink. I've no desire to know what anybody else wants to do. I don't do this to influence young people. I do this because, you know, I don't do it. I think that people should make up their own minds about the things in life. I think that perhaps they're advised too much in too many things.

Some people say I'm over the top of the hill. I think it's important to be looking up the hill, so I'm turning my back and looking up the hill and coming down backwards, if this is the case.

DANNY BLANCHFLOWER

LORD SHAWCROSS

I think the lawyer in politics has a difficult position. A lawyer is, of course, by training, apt to speak from a brief and if he speaks simply from a brief as an advocate, he's not being sincere. If, on the other hand, he's being sincere, his legal training is also a disadvantage because he tends to see both sides of the question and a really successful politician, I'm sure, should only see one side and believe passionately in that side, and I've never managed quite to do that.

I was very partisan in those days. I was full of enthusiasm and lacking in experience and I dropped the most frightful clangers, I know that, and they were a great source of terror to me. I dreaded seeing the Monday morning newspapers as much as anybody, but on the whole, I think I had a genuine belief in most of the things that I said, although I'm afraid I often said them in a way which was calculated to lead to trouble.

I'm completely in favour of the abolition of capital punishment. I don't think there's any evidence at all that it's an effective deterrent. I think that the practice of the death penalty is demoralizing and reduces respect for human life.

If your personal convictions clash with your brief, being at the Bar would drive you mad very quickly. I think you develop an attitude of mind in which you become completely detached from any personal view about the rights or wrongs of the case you're appearing in. Sometimes I remember I did have a very strong personal conviction that somebody for whom I was appearing was right or wrong. That was a very worrying thing and made one terribly upset and anxious.

I intended originally to be a doctor. I actually got to the point of entering myself in a hospital, but I had to wait some time before I could get a place in the hospital, I remember. I was out at Geneva filling in time. I was supposed to be a student at the university there, when the first meeting of the Socialist International, after the First World War, took place. I'd already joined the Labour Party and I thought it'd be rather fun to attend this, and so I offered my services as an interpreter. I was duly appointed as an interpreter and there I got to know some of the leaders of the Labour Party, including Ramsay Macdonald and that great character J. H. Thomas. He thought it was rather amusing that this comparatively young boy should be acting as an interpreter and he took me a little under his wing and he said, 'Well, if you want to go into politics it's no good being a doctor. You won't have the time. The Bar's the thing.' And so I went to the Bar. I think I have regretted that decision. I think medicine is an extraordinarily satisfying profession. Must be, and I never, I'm afraid, felt quite the same about the Bar. I dare say I'd have been a very bad doctor, but I think one must get more personal satisfaction out of curing somebody from disease than out of prosecuting someone and sending him to prison.

I'm sorry to hear there are any of my school records at all. The first time I went back to Dulwich after leaving was when I went as chairman of the Governors. I should have thought that my records would have disqualified me.

When I was in Parliament and never went home at night, I remember one of my children saying that he didn't know his father. That affected me very much because I have had a very happy home life and I value it tremendously and I'm very fond of my children. They behave disgracefully but I enjoy it.

Augustus JOHN

There are three large things on the wall, on which I've been working a lot lately, but what they mean—I give up! But they really start, in a sense, from one's knowledge of European painting—say, Giotto. He had a large following down to the grand Renaissance of Michelangelo, Raphael, Leonardo —I haven't got to them. That's the most elaborate composition of the lot, done without models, except for one. I've not finished it. There are some, probably about twenty, wonderful painters who are not usually heard of, after Giotto. Duccio, for one. These influences are noticeable—I *hope* they're noticeable—which explains perhaps my general attitude towards painting now. I'd like to go on from where Giotto stopped, if it were possible. I'm a good deal more industrious than I used to be. I think I used to daydream a lot. Now I can't afford to do that. I'm not a fashionable portrait painter, I much prefer painting my friends and people I happen to meet. Painting, in my view, is a visual experience, not abstract— visual. That's what interests one. Inspiration is all very well but it's hard work which makes the difference. One is excited over certain aspects of life more than others and one becomes so to speak inflamed. In that case it's quite possible one might do better than otherwise. She was a very good model and a very interesting girl. She draws, herself, very well. A very well-known French painter got me to paint him. He writes too —or did. He's dead. His name? Well, it escapes me at the moment but he was extremely well-known. That's a portrait of some young girl I used to know. As you see, it's unfinished. The human body does interest me. At the Slade I made a kind of reputation as a draughtsman of the figure and head. You see that one—I don't know whether you've noticed it—it bears some

faint resemblance to myself—painting. I discovered it—or rediscovered it, recently, in the cellar over there among other things. I hauled it out. I thought it might interest people, and so it did. I used to draw as a child. I have no results of that period left, thank God! But I did have a desire to draw.

I'm a Welshman—a bad Welshman. But I was brought up in a non-Welsh-speaking part — South Pembrokeshire — where no word of Welsh is heard.

I was born in Tenby. My parents were there on a visit. Their home was Haverfordwest.

My father once drew up a list of my misdeeds at school, accusing me of having punched one of my masters. This was quite true. I did! He asked for it. So he then took a stick and applied it to my behind, not half hard enough. I rushed out of the room laughing violently.

This master came behind me one day and hit me with one of these little rulers—hard ruler, you know. I punched him back. It was very well directed! In the right spot. I can remember one thing in an early school in Tenby. I'd practically idolized one of the masters, as schoolboys are apt to do, I think, and he betrayed me and held me up before the whole school, denounced me as a liar, d'you see, and the fact was I was completely innocent. I made a mistake, I know, a formal matter, but instead of protesting I succumbed before the class. I never forgave that man and I'm very glad to be able to report that soon after he blew his brains out, you see—in a railway train. I think I must have put something on him.

My father? I'd rather not go very far in that. I think of his family he was the only successful one. He had brothers, also, as far as I remember, occupied with the law, but he was the one who made good at it.

Respectability was his slogan. Well, he was a good churchman, that is to say he attended church religiously—or at any rate, every Sunday. Oh, yes, he was respected, all right.

My father decided when his wife died—my mother—I saw very little of her. She was much of an invalid, unfortunately, and used to be away taking cures in spas or things like that. The poor woman hadn't much of a good time, and when it came—I remember her death being announced and my poor father in a ghastly hurry catching a train to see about this. But I do remember her at moments, all the same.

I've no direct knowledge of God. I can't pretend to know him very well. Well, which god? There are so many, it seems. The more you read anthropology the more gods you have to consider. They all seem to me to be pretty good in their various lights.

I went to the Slade, I should think, when I was about fourteen or fifteen. . . . Occasionally I went to the theatre or something like that, you know. And then I had a craze for diet. I'd only eat nuts and fruit. No vegetables, no bread. But it was a little dull, you know. Sometimes one was asked out to dinner or something and one had a good blow-out, you see.

My beard grew by itself! I never stopped it. It's a virgin beard. I think it was brown. My father was ginger-headed, used to be, but I didn't inherit that. No wonder they called me Jesus Christ! The little boys in the street, the horrid little boys.

I met my wife at the Slade. She was a fellow student, and we married shortly afterwards. We were really poor. And then we got an offer to go to Liverpool to run a school of drawing and painting and that helped. I went to Liverpool and enjoyed it very much. I should think we lived there about two years, or perhaps three—I'm not sure about that. I'm very bad about dates. Our eldest boy was born there. We had four or five. And one was—she lost one. We lost one. Poor boy; he was a brilliant boy and he died bathing in Cornwall. Wonderful fellow.

My first wife was having a baby and she went to a French place for that, you know, and unfortunately I don't think it was very well looked after. She got an appalling condition and then she had to go to a hospital where I used to go and see her—every day, I think—and there unfortunately the poor girl expired. We had a friend who came and made herself indispensable and looked after the children.

Certainly I'm interested in women. In beauty, I should think. If it's beauty, it's love. In my case! You've got to get excited before you can do anything, and beauty is a great excitant.

I was always interested in gypsies, even as a child, but I was frightened. I was told that they ran off with other people's children. Considering they had plenty of their own I can't believe that. But I was told to avoid them, by my nurses. I was always fascinated by them as a child, seeing them in the markets at Haverfordwest, strange foreign people. And then when I got to Liverpool I fell in with a great friend we made, John Samson, who was a student of Romany, and we went about a lot together. There I learnt the fine dialect spoken by one tribe in the north.

I've never voted in my life so far. I am interested, but at a certain distance, but I'm not devoted to either party—or any party. It's a lack of interest. No doubt both parties contain admirable people but I don't have to spoil my slate at this time of life by voting at all.

I think I've got a very fishy reputation—as a painter—because I'm out of date. I don't do abstractions.

I don't think the R.A.'s changed a bit but it's the cheapest place. You don't have to pay anything. They don't have a rake-off. I resigned over a picture by Lewis that I hadn't seen, and they rejected it, and knowing Lewis I thought they should have hung it, you know—theoretically. When I saw the picture I thought they were quite right to have chucked it out . . . I was re-elected. They've always been very decent to me, although I haven't been a very great supporter of it.

I read *The Times* and the *Chronicle*.

I grudge every hour when it's impossible to work.

I should be ashamed of wasting my time. I've wasted a good deal, I imagine, thinking that life went on almost for ever.

A painter leaves his emotion behind, which other people can share.

I knew it was a great distinction to get the Order of Merit, and I thanked them for it, whoever they were. But I wasn't oppressed by that grandeur.

I like success, occasionally.

Yes, I'd like to have my life all over, because I enjoyed it so, with its unhappiness too, thrown in.

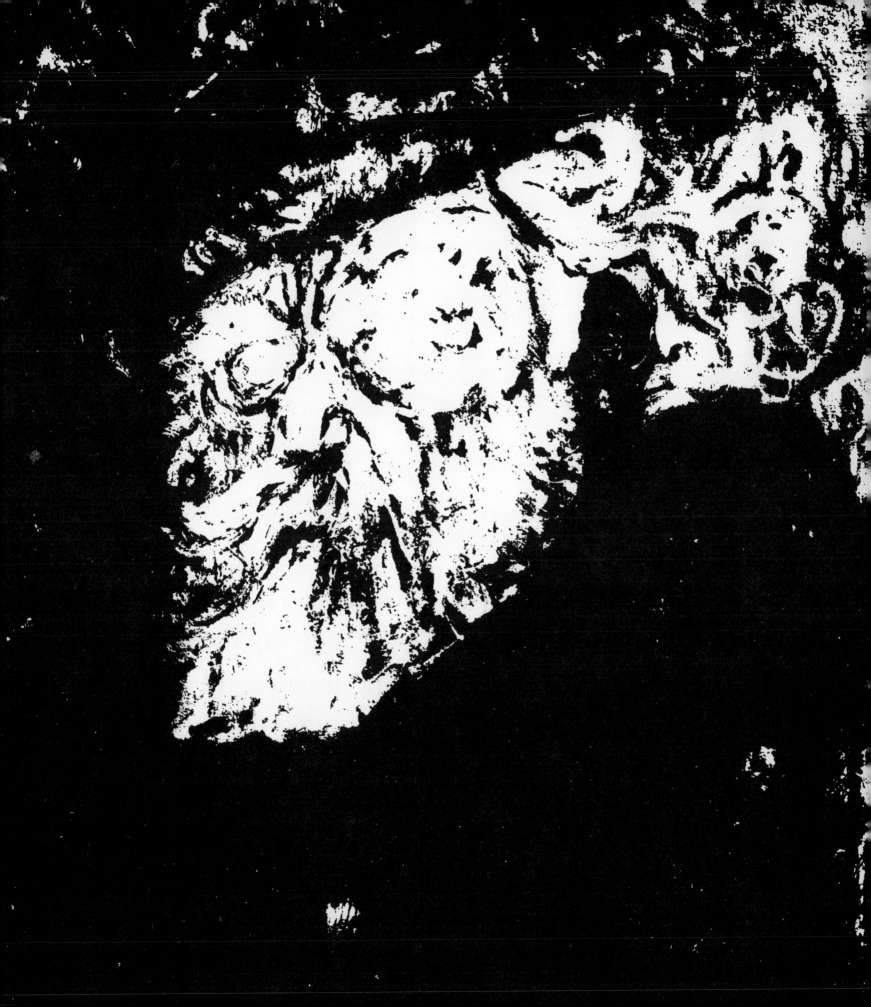

Carl Gustav JUNG

In my eleventh year, there I suddenly was, on my way to school—I stepped out of a mist. It was just as if I had been in a mist, walking in a mist, and I stepped out of it and I knew, 'I am.' 'I am what I am.' And then I thought, 'But what have I been before?' And then I found that I had been in a mist, not knowing how to differentiate myself from things. I was just one thing among many things.

My parents belonged to the later part of the Middle Ages. My father was a parson in the country and you can imagine what people were then, you know, in the seventies of the past century. They had the convictions in which people have lived since one thousand eight hundred years.

My father was very liberal, and he was most tolerant and most understanding. Of course, one is always more intimate with the mother, but when it comes to the personal feeling, I had a better relation to my father, who was predictable, than with my mother, who was to me a very problematical something. I knew he was very fallible. Perhaps when I was eleven or twelve years old. It was hanging together with the fact that I knew I *was*, and from then on I saw that my father was different. But I realized that I had fear of my mother. But not during the day. Then she was quite known to me, and predictable, but in the night I had fear of my mother. I have not the slightest idea why.

In the beginning at school I was very happy to have companions, because before I had been very lonely. We lived in the country and I had no brother and no sister. My sister was born very much later, when I was nine years old, and so I was used to be alone. But I missed company, and in school it was wonderful to have company. But soon—you know in a country school naturally I was far ahead—and then I began to be bored.

We were Swiss Reformed. Everybody went to church on Sunday.

Do I now believe in God? Difficult to answer. I know. *I don't need to believe. I know.*

Originally I wanted to be an archaeologist; Assyriology, Egyptology or something of the sort. I hadn't the money; the study was too expensive. So my second love then belonged to nature, particularly zoology, and when I began my studies I inscribed in the so-called philosophical faculty, too— that means natural sciences—but then I soon saw that to pass my—the career that was before me would make a schoolmaster of me. But I never thought I had any chance to get any further, because we had no money at all. And then I saw that that didn't suit my expectations, you know. I didn't want to become a schoolmaster. Teaching was not just what I was looking for. And so I remembered that my grandfather had been a doctor, and I knew that when I was studying medicine I had a chance to study natural science and to become a doctor. And a doctor can develop, you see, he can have a practice, he can choose his scientific interests more or less. At all events I would have more chance than being a schoolmaster. And the idea of doing something useful with human beings appealed to me.

I particularly had a difficulty with certain teachers. They didn't believe that I could write a thesis. I remember one case where the teacher had the custom, the habit, to discuss the papers written by the pupils, and he took the best first. And he went through the whole number of the pupils and I didn't appear. I was badly troubled over it, and I thought well, it is impossible that my thesis can be *that* bad. When he had finished he said, 'There is still one paper left over and that is the one by Jung. That would be by far the best paper if it hadn't been copied. He has just copied this somewhere—stolen! You are a thief, Jung. And if I knew where you had stolen it I would fling you out of school!" And I got mad and said this is the one thesis where I have worked the most, because the theme was interesting, in contradistinction you know, to other themes which are not at all interesting to me. And then he said, 'You are a liar, and if we can prove that you have stolen that thing somewhere, then you get out of school.' Now that was a very serious thing to me, because what else then, you see? And I hated that fellow. That was the only man I could have killed, you know, if I had met him once at a dark corner! I would have shown him something of what I could do.

JUNG *cont'd*

I was pretty strong, and reared in the country with those peasant boys. It was a rough kind of life. I would have been capable of violence, I know. I was a bit afraid of it, so I rather tried to avoid critical situations because I didn't trust myself. Once I was attacked by about seven boys and I got mad, and I took one, and just swung him round with his legs and beat down four of them. Then they were satisfied. From then on it was always suspected that I was at the bottom of every trouble. I was not, but they were afraid and I was never attacked again.

When I had finished my studies practically and when I didn't know what I really wanted to do, I had a big chance to follow one of my professors. He was called to a new position in Munich, and he wanted me as his assistant. But then in that moment I studied for my final examination, I came across a textbook of psychiatry. Up to then I thought nothing about it, because our professor wasn't particularly interested in it. And I only read the introduction to that book, where certain things were said, about psychosis as a maladjustment of the personality. That hit the nail on the head. In that moment I saw I must become an alienist. My heart was thumping wildly in that moment, and when I told my professor I wouldn't follow him, I would study psychiatry, he couldn't understand it. Nor my friends, because in those days psychiatry was nothing, nothing at all. But I saw the one great chance to unite certain contrasting things in myself, namely, beside natural science I always had studied history of philosophy and such subjects. It was just as if suddenly two streams were joining.

It took quite a while until I met Freud. You see, I'd finished my studies in 1900 and I met Freud altogether much later. I read—in 1900—I already read his *Dream Interpretation* and Breuer's and Freud's *Studies on Hysteria*, but that was merely literary, and then in 1907 I became acquainted with him personally. I'd written a book about the psychology of dementia praecox, schizophrenia then. And I sent him that book, and thus became acquainted. I went to Vienna for a fortnight and then we had a very long and penetrating conversation, and that settled it. It soon developed into a personal friendship. He was a complicated nature, you know. I liked him very much, but I soon discovered that when he had thought something

then it was settled, while I was doubting all along the line, and it was impossible to discuss something really *au fond*. You know he had no philosophical education, particularly—I was studying Kant, and I was steeped in it and that was far from Freud. So from the very beginning there was a discrepancy.

There is always a temperamental difference, and his approach was naturally different from mine because his personality was different from mine. That led me into my later investigation of psychological types, with definite attitudes. Some people are doing it in this way and other people are doing it in another *typical* way, and there were such differences between myself and Freud, too. . . . From the beginning I had certain reservations; I couldn't agree with quite a number of his ideas, chiefly, his purely personal approach, and his disregard of the historical conditions of man. You see, we depend largely upon our history. We are shaped through education, through the influence of the parents, which are by no means always personal. They were prejudiced, or they were influenced by historical ideas or what are called dominants, and that is a most decisive factor in psychology. We are not of today or of yesterday; we are of an immense age.

I submitted quite a lot of my dreams to him, and so did he to me.

It was partly my experience with schizophrenic patients that led me to the idea of certain general historical conditions. I made quite a number of experiences of that sort and I went even to Washington to study negroes at the psychiatric clinic there, in order to find out whether they had the same type of dreams as we have, and these experiences and others led me then to the hypothesis that there is an impersonal stratum in our psyche, and I can tell you an example. We had a patient in the ward; he was quiet but completely dissociated, a schizophrenic, and he was in the clinic or the ward twenty years. He had come into the clinic as a matter of fact a young man, a little clerk and with no particular education, and once I came into the ward and he was obviously excited and called to me, took me by the lapel of my coat, and led me to the window, and said: 'Doctor! Now! Now you will see. Now look at it. Look up at the sun and see how it moves.

See, you must move your head, too, like this, and then you will see the phallus of the sun, and you know, that's the origin of the wind. And you see how the sun moves, as you move your head, from one side to the other!' Of course, I did not understand it at all. I thought oh, there you are, he's just crazy. But that case remained in my mind. And four years later I came across a paper written by the German historian, Dieterich, who had dealt with the so-called Mithras Liturgy, a part of the great Parisian source of papyrus, which said, 'After the second prayer thou wilt see the disc of the sun unfold, and you will see hanging down from it the tube, the origin of the wind, and when you move thy face to the regions of the east it will move there, and if you move your face to the region of the west it will follow you.' And instantly I knew now—that is it! *This* is the vision of my patient! And that thing was not known. It was in a magic papyrus in Paris, and it wasn't even published. It was only published four years later, after I had observed it with my patient.

This was not a proof to me, but it was a hint. And I took the hint.

My own psychological type is nothing static. It changes in the course of life, but I most certainly was characterized by thinking. I always thought, from early childhood on, and I had a great deal of intuition too, and I had a definite difficulty with feeling, and my relation to reality was not particularly brilliant. I was often at variance with the reality of things. That gives you all the necessary data for a diagnosis!

We need more psychology. We need more understanding of human nature, because the only real danger that exists is man itself. He is the great danger, and we are pitifully unaware of it. We know nothing of man, far too little. His psyche should be studied, because we are the origin of all coming evil.

I don't believe that man will ever deviate from the original pattern of his being.

We are not quite certain about the end of our lives. Quite honestly, one cannot be quite certain about it, because you know there are these peculiar faculties of the psyche, that it isn't entirely confined to space and time; you can have dreams or visions of the future, you can see around corners and such things. Only ignorance denies these facts, you know; it's quite evident that they do exist, and have existed always. Now these facts show that the psyche, in part at least, is not dependent upon these confinements. And then what? When the psyche is not under that obligation to live in time and space alone, and obviously it doesn't, then to that extent the psyche is not subjected to those laws, and that means a practical continuation of life, of a sort of psychical existence beyond time and space.

The word belief is a difficult thing for me. I don't believe. I must have a reason for a certain hypothesis. Either I know a thing, and then I know it. I don't need to believe it—I don't allow myself, for instance, to believe a thing just for the sake of believing it. I can't believe it, but when there are sufficient reasons for a certain hypothesis, I shall accept naturally. And I should say, 'We had to reckon with the possibility of so and so.'

I have treated many old people and it's quite interesting to watch what the unconscious is doing with the fact that it is apparently threatened with a complete end. It disregards it. Life behaves as if it were going on, and so I think it is better for an old person to live on, to look forward to the next day, as if he had to spend centuries, and then he lives properly. But when he is afraid, when he doesn't look forward, he looks back, he petrifies, he gets stiff and he dies before his time. But when he's living on, looking forward to the great adventure that is ahead, then he lives, and that is about what the unconscious is intending to do. Of course, it's quite obvious that we're all going to die, and this is the sad finale of everything, but nevertheless, there is something in us that doesn't believe it apparently. But this is merely a fact, a psychological fact—it doesn't mean to me that it proves something. It is simply so. For instance, I may not know why we need salt, but we prefer to eat salt, too, because we feel better. And so when you think in a certain way you may feel considerably better, and I think if you think along the lines of nature then you think properly.

Man will not stand for ever his nullification. There will be a reaction, and I see it setting in. When I think of my patients, they all seek their own existence and to assure their existence against that complete atomization into nothingness, or into meaninglessness. Man cannot stand a meaningless life.

JOHN HUSTON

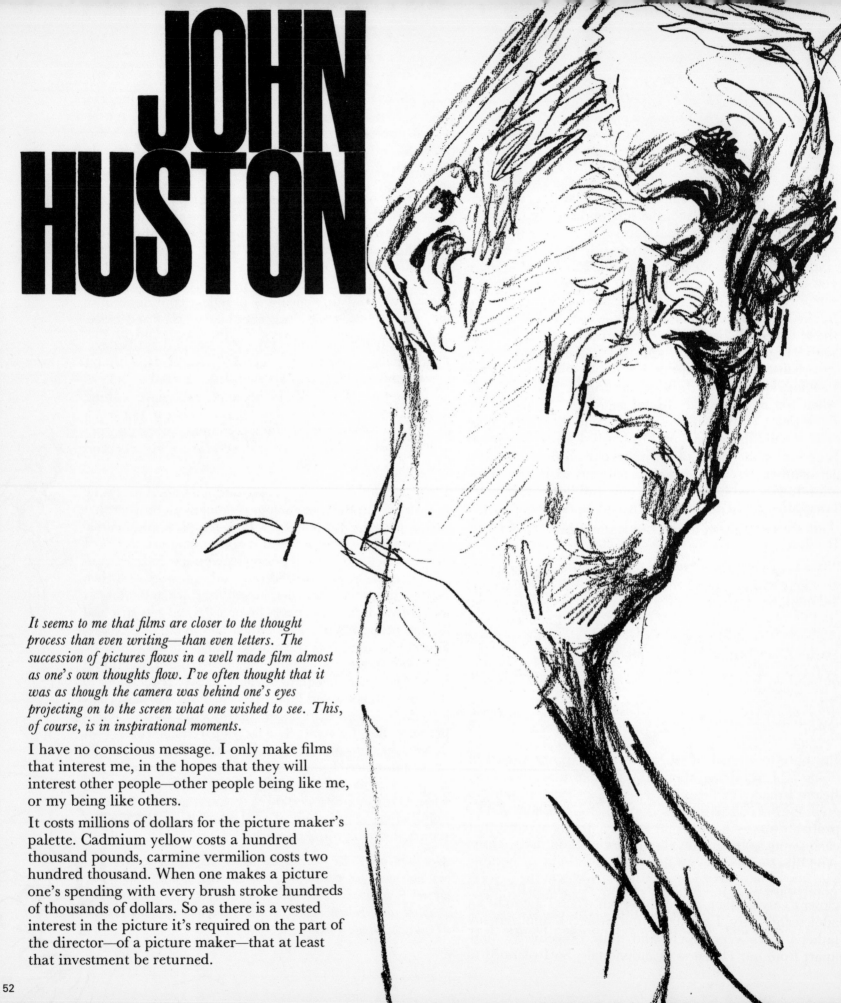

It seems to me that films are closer to the thought process than even writing—than even letters. The succession of pictures flows in a well made film almost as one's own thoughts flow. I've often thought that it was as though the camera was behind one's eyes projecting on to the screen what one wished to see. This, of course, is in inspirational moments.

I have no conscious message. I only make films that interest me, in the hopes that they will interest other people—other people being like me, or my being like others.

It costs millions of dollars for the picture maker's palette. Cadmium yellow costs a hundred thousand pounds, carmine vermilion costs two hundred thousand. When one makes a picture one's spending with every brush stroke hundreds of thousands of dollars. So as there is a vested interest in the picture it's required on the part of the director—of a picture maker—that at least that investment be returned.

I wanted to make *The Red Badge of Courage* and they didn't want me to make it. So I brought pressure—only psychological pressure—I pursued it, and asked them again to let me make it, and a third and a fourth time, and finally they agreed, and much against their wills. And I made it, and I made it to my satisfaction, and I shall never forget the first night—or rather the preview, what they call a sneak preview—I shall never forget the people rising, and the audience rising and walking out of the theatre. I swear they'd have fought their way to get out. They didn't like it. They liked no part of it.

I made a film for the American army. I was in the army and it was the last work I did before going out of uniform. It was not censored. It was simply not shown. I think the main reason was their reluctance to invade the privacy of these men who were neurotics and who after the making of the film—as a matter of fact during the making of the film—recovered, at least, to their former state of emotional composure. It's no great advertisement for war to see what the experience of combat does to men's souls.

My very good friend, Errol Flynn, and I—we weren't friends then—there's no better way to get friends with a man than to have a fight with him—we were at a party. I stopped to have a drink with Errol, and Errol said something rather objectionable about a friend of mine. I think I called him a dirty name for that and said it was untrue and even if it was true, why, he was a dirty name for repeating it. Errol said, 'Do you want to make anything out of it?' This is total recall. And I said, 'Yes.' So we went down to the bottom of the garden and the party went on, and we fought—a long, excellent, very, very good fight it was—fought for the better part of an hour, and then it was discovered that the fight was going on. They came out and we were separated and went to the hospital, our various ways.

Ambition has turned sour on me, I think probably five days out of the week.

I'm only interested in what I'm doing at the time I'm doing it. I'm talking about film-making now, of course. Before I made my first film, a very dear friend of mine, a great film-maker named Henry Blankey, of whom you've probably never heard, said to me, 'John, be sure that each scene, as you make it, is the best scene in the picture.' And this I've tried to observe.

My parents divorced when I was about six. I was probably closer to my mother, as a child is, but when I got to be an adolescent, why I went to my father. I admired my father's work very much, and quite objectively, quite apart from our closeness as individuals. So I planned to make films in which I thought my father could shine. He was a very strong man, character-wise. And a very moral man. I don't mean moral in any bigoted or small sense but only in the larger sense. I don't think my father ever committed an unfaithful and untrue act in his life.

When I was about eleven years old, they took me to Arizona for my health, and I was like all children anxious for that, yearning for that physical freedom that was denied to me. And I didn't have any better sense than, at night, when the room was asleep and the house was quiet, to slip out. And I used to go swimming in the canals, the canals of Phoenix.

Once in London, when I was about twenty-five years old, a whole series of circumstances mounted up to my finally being completely broke and without much hope of being otherwise. I could have called to my father for help or friends. But I'm enough of a believer in the gambler's creed that if you're in a bad streak there's nothing to do about it. You've just got to play it out. And so for six months I slept on the Embankment and in such thresholds and beds as were offered. And at the end of the six months the luck turned.

I suppose I mind about my children more than anything else in the world. They are a projection of me. I'm trying to make them better than I am, which is the hope of every father, I'm sure. I look for my future in them.

Oh, I think that the thing that is really lacking is a sense of purpose, you know. There's not much point in asking people whether they're coal heavers from Wigan, or chimney sweepers from Stoke-on-Trent, nor even in answering questions from Dimbleby and Train on whether the object is animal, vegetable or mineral. But it keeps one out of the workhouse, you know.

The thing I do better than anything else is teach. I was a very good schoolmaster, a very good teacher, but I couldn't go into that again now, could I? Nobody would employ me. I shouldn't be able to live on the salary, either.

I've never done anything that was physically exhausting because I've never been physically very competent.

I drifted into teaching when I became a Papist. There was nothing else to do.

I terrified the little boys—either by shouting or looking terrible.

I became a policeman because I was fed up with being a schoolmaster and it seemed to me to be an escape. I didn't intend to be a police constable on the beat for all that time. I thought that I might, with a Cambridge degree, however squalid, shabby, third-class—you know, three-three—I thought I might become an education officer or something, or even become a detective, and that would have been very nice. But then I broke my knee. I had a cartilage disturbance and that was inconvenient and troublesome and in the middle of all that I was offered a job in Cyprus, so I went.

When I was a recruit I had to do a lot of hopping about, vaulting over horses and things like that, and keeping fit, which I've always disliked very much. And then I was on that awful shift which begins at six o'clock in the evening and ends at two o'clock in the morning. It wasn't very amusing, going round and seeing whether people had locked up their premises or not. It wasn't exciting.

I didn't like the helmet. That's why I was hoping to get into the motor squad where I could have worn a flat cap.

I think I do like life in big institutions. I've often thought I'd like to join a monastery, but then I'd have to behave myself much more than I'm able to do. I think I'm happier when I'm with a lot of other people.

Gilbert Harding

I never thought of administering discipline! I'm always rather afraid of being subject to it. I never thought of administering it. Do I like bossing other people about? I suppose I do really. Yes, I never thought of it. M'm. It is rather pleasant to have people jumping about—only every now and then!

I think about pain every now and then when I read about it. When I read about it I find it rather frightening. I can stay with people if they're suffering pain but I loathe the idea of State infliction or anything of that sort. I dislike it very much. The anonymous indeterminate authority which directs that people should be punished is awful. The same as I read sometimes about the agonies of people under examination and brainwashing. Any kind of torture makes me feel quite ill.

I must have a few enemies. I'm not aware of many. There are only two or three people in the world I dislike, and I think I've on the whole got more friends than enemies. I think. Occasionally if I dislike two people very much I feel it would serve them right to be alone together for a long time and have to put up with one another's conversation.

I've never consciously striven for success, but once I was aware I had it I must say that I'm terrified of losing it. I wouldn't like nowadays, at my advanced age and with all the sensitivities and miseries that have come upon me, I wouldn't like to be shown up for instance.

I dream constantly. Anxieties and impossible situations. On the whole I'm the sort of suffering figure. I dream about unpleasant situations in which I might have been in and got out of and my dreams are that I didn't get out of them and they developed horribly. Sometimes I remember them, sometimes I don't.

My mother was always a sort of comforting and on the whole rather over-ready source of assuagement and there was always a sort of bosom to cry on. She had a sort of patient smile and resigned shrugging of shoulders, as much as to say, well, I shall never understand you but I suppose you know what you're doing—a rather tired and weary woman. I didn't like my sister very much. She's dead too. I didn't get on with her very well.

As a child I was abominably badly behaved. I remember throwing things about and creating scenes and tearing things up and smashing plates and pretending to be ill when I wasn't and making my temperature go up and attracting sympathy and things of that sort, which after a time she got, as they say in America, wise to, and that didn't work any more. So I had to think of something else.

My sister didn't marry and I didn't marry and my mother was a widow just when she was thirty, and so when we came to live together we put up a sort of cloud of sexual frustration that was enough to blot out the sun, and I've never been particularly affectionate. One of my troubles is that I don't attract affection very much and when I do I tend to repel it. I'm not a sort of intimate or cosy person.

I don't really like living in close contact with anybody. I like to think that it's because I realize I'm almost unfit to live with, but that's probably giving myself the benefit of thinking that I'm largely unselfish. I think I'm pretty difficult to live with.

I'm profoundly lonely.

I'm not afraid of death. I'm afraid of dying. I should be very glad to be dead, but I don't look forward to the actual process of dying.

When one's very ill I find that one doesn't think of dying. Afterwards, when people tell you how ill you've been, in my case, at least, I feel why on earth did they bother. It would have been very much better to have let me go. That, of course, is very mean; I should feel very grateful to them.

I'd much rather be dead than alive if I hadn't got to go through the miseries of actually dying.

I've no fear of hell, and purgatory won't be all that bad.

Religion to me is a *daily* force. It's not as active as it should be. Sometimes holidays and Sundays are overlooked, and then I always have an excuse. I'm not very well. I'm lazy and dishonest about that.

Confession gives relief and satisfaction and refreshment.

I've started being psycho-analysed—once or twice—but never gone on with it. I don't think it's for me. I'm sure that psychiatrists are able to help lots of people but I think they have to be ready to be helped and willing and pliant, and I'm not very willing and not very pliant and not very convinced. Therefore I think it's on the whole a waste of their time and of mine. Yes, I've felt the need for it. I'd like somebody to tell me how to behave better, but after all I know that. And the best psycho-analysts really are priests.

My bad manners and bad temper are quite indefensible, but I'm never willingly rude to people, people who as you say can't answer back or can't stand up—never willingly—I quite often am, I suppose, by accident. I'm always very sorry and say so. But I quite often lose my temper and am very rude to people who are in a much better position to answer back, and they often do.

I lack companionship, security and a sense of purpose.

Gilbert Harding

OTTO KLEMPERER

When I was six years, my mother gave me piano lessons. She had been a professional piano teacher and I made some progress, but I was not good. So they took a teacher, who was strict with me. It was then all right. At first I was always very much interested in the theatre, and I thought I'd become an actor. They all said I should become a musician, but I wanted to be an actor. That was my idea, but fortunately at sixteen I left school. Then I went to the Conservatory in Frankfurt. At first, I took a lot of piano lessons with the Dutch pianist James Kwast, and theory with a good teacher, Ivan Knorr. I was so happy to be there and to be out of school, because I hated school.

My favourite subjects were history, languages—Latin and French and English. But not zoology and mathematics. I didn't care for that.

I was pretty serious as a boy I think. At first I exercised the piano, maybe eight hours every day. I intended to become a pianist, and I became it. I learned also a little violin, but only a little bit.

I always wanted to be a conductor. I had a very amusing occasion in 1906—Max Reinhardt gave the *Orpheus in the Underworld* of Offenbach, and he engaged Oscar Fried, at that time a very famous conductor, to conduct it. And there was some trouble between him and the first singer and I conducted it for fifty evenings. I was very proud. Then it was decided that I became a conductor. I was twenty-one.

I had had some experience in the Conservatory. I conducted the orchestra of the Conservatory, but only in minor things. And then—my greatest impression at that time was the conductor, Mahler. I heard him conduct in Vienna the *Walküre* and *Iphigénie in Aulis* at a concert—it was wonderful; it was very, very great. Today we speak always of the enormous greatness of Toscanini—I assure you Mahler was much greater. I met him first in Berlin. Then Oscar Fried conducted the second symphony and I had the honour to conduct the little orchestra behind stage. And then I made a piano transcription for two hands of the second symphony and showed it to him in Vienna and he gave me a recommendation, very good recommendation, which I have still today, and this opened all doors to me. He was my spiritus rector, he was very good to me. I came then,

by his recommendation, to Prague, as a real conductor, and I stayed there for three years. Then I went, also by his recommendation, to Hamburg, and I stayed there also about three years, then came a little intermission in Barmen in the Wuppertal. I was there one year and then I came to Strasbourg, for three years, and came to Cologne, seven years. I married a singer, my wife, and we had the two children. Then came '33 and then I was forced to go away.

Walter is a very good conductor, but he is an absolutely other character than I am. You see it's difficult to speak about this. He is very conciliating and very elegant, and very mild, and I am not. He is very romantic; I am not at all. And he is what we call—but you must not misunderstand—he is a moralist and I am an immoralist. Absolutely.

We went to Zürich in Switzerland and to Vienna because I hoped Hitler would stop in Germany, not go to Austria. Then I saw that he came to Austria too, so we went over to America. I am very grateful to America because she gave me and my family bread and work. The orchestras in America are very good. I mean the orchestras in the east, the Boston, the Philadelphia, the New York Philharmonic, very good, the best in the world. But I don't like the dollar—always the dollar!

At first I became Musical Director of the Philharmonic Orchestra in Los Angeles. That was in '33, and then in '39 I became very ill. I had a brain tumour, and it was necessary to operate it in Boston. Fortunately this became better but in the whole year I was out of my work, and then I did not get again Musical Director—I was guest conductor.

I hated Germany—I was so furious about this attitude against us, against born Jews, that I naturally took American citizenship, but I gave it up. In '54 we went to Europe, and I was undecided whether I should go back to America or stay in Europe. But then I find out that every two years one must come and stay a little bit in the United States, every two years, back and forth, that was too expensive. So I said to the German authorities I will become German again, and they were very happy, and in three days it was all right. And now I have a passport, I can travel wherever I want. Also to Budapest, or to Moscow—I can travel. Now I am a German who lives in a foreign country.

This is my home where I can work at best—so my second Fatherland is really England. But in vacation time I go back to Zürich and that's very good for resting. It is necessary for an artist to have some kind of relaxation—he cannot always work. Germany I refuse to go back to, and so Switzerland. Austria is very fine but the east is not very good. Zürich is very nice. Big lake, and many trees, and in summertime you can go always up in the mountains to the Engadine, to St Moritz, and that's wonderful—unique.

I fractured my hip in '51. The most serious event was in, I think, '58. I was burning—third degree. My life was in great danger although I didn't know it. I went to bed and took my pipe. I don't know what happened. It came together with the wool of the curtain. I had on my night table a little bottle of alcohol because I had a little pain, and I thought with alcohol the fire will be out. But on the contrary it was very high and then I was pretty lost. And then my daughter wakened by accident, and she came to my room, and all the covers were alight. It was most unhappy.

A man can conduct with the hand, but mostly one conducts with the eyes. And sitting—my goodness in the opera the conductors are always sitting. And the concert does not have it, but it's just the same. One doesn't conduct with the leg. One conducts with the arms and with the eyes. That's the most important.

This orchestra—the Philharmonia —is all my joy. The orchestra has really developed. We have a lot of new people there and they are very good, and they are very good to me, so I am also very good to them. They play very good for me. English audiences are very fair.

I read again and again Goethe and Shakespeare and Heine. If I am very tired I like to read Nietzsche—that's my favourite writer. I think he's wonderful.

I have composed my whole life, and do it today as I did it sixty years before. I have very few works published—there's a mass published by Schotts in Mayence, and some songs, but I hope it will become more.

In nature I am very much up and down—up and down, and between these two is naturally very difficult. But, generally, it is all right. This up and down is—thanks to God—less in the last years, because then I am older and more quiet, and so. . . .

HANCOCK

I think the world is both funny and sad, which seem to me to be the two basic ingredients of good comedy.

The character I play isn't a character I put on and off like a coat. It is a part of me and a part of everybody else I see.

The secret of my work is a knowledge of what constitutes living in general, I think. You take the weaknesses of your own character and of other people's characters and you exploit them. You show yourself up and you show them up.

I have no religion now. I'm deeply interested and I'm trying to find a faith. But I've had to throw away the initial faith that I was brought up in and therefore am now starting again from scratch. I began to see first when I was about fifteen or sixteen. I think I was fairly deeply Christian before that and it just failed. It was no longer believable.

The only use I have for money really is to travel and to have the luxury of independence to choose what work I do and to read and to learn, and to put something back into my own profession. The two things go together. The more you expand as an individual, the more you see, the more you read, the more you learn, the more you have to offer.

I love France. I find it very relaxing. I relax there better than anywhere, I think, partly because of the licensing laws. People say why do you go to Paris to rest? But I do rest there, because you can go to sleep six hours in the afternoon, you can get up and go out all night if you want to.

I read history, philosophy, and all the things that come off it. It seems as if for the first thirty years my eyes were closed and then I became interested and found a real thirst for knowledge, and now I fortunately have the opportunity to put right this lack of education. Once I read Wells's *Outline of History*. Simple, maybe, but it put the thing into perspective. It put one into an entirely different position. Viewing your own sort of ego and personality in terms of this vast time. That really started me reading many other things.

I'm entirely interested in comedy. I read practically all the newspapers. I also think it's necessary to watch nearly all television, for instance. It's hard to bear, isn't it? If you want to see something that needs burlesquing or something you want to have a go at, you have to see it all.

Reluctantly I read the critics' opinions of myself. That hurts. I try and eliminate that but it's not possible. You think about the point anybody makes. It would be nice to say you were beyond that, maybe, but you never are.

Sometimes I spend money extravagantly. I like staying at big hotels in a suite occasionally for a couple of days. I like to travel, to travel in considerable luxury, maybe.

Generally I don't sleep well, and take sleeping pills.

I don't worry much about my weight. I've got it more or less sorted out now. Well, within reason. I was about two-and-a-half stone heavier than this at one time. For a time I diet and then after a show is over, after a series is over, I do anything, whatever I want, and then I pull right down. I think being fat makes you sluggish generally. Your mind is sluggish and I think that's a bad thing.

My father was rather like me in a way. He had a lot of moods, he did all sorts of things. He was a laundry owner, a pub-keeper, a hotel keeper, a boxing referee—all sorts—also a semi-pro comedian. He fluctuated a great deal.

My names Anthony Aloysius St John are not true. They were created by the scriptwriters. My real name is Anthony John Hancock.

My father and mother tried to give me the best education they possibly could, which I think was a fine thing for them to do because neither of them had an education really, you know, and I didn't want it. I felt being at a public school was making the thing too much in a mould, and I left there myself at fifteen. It was one of the best decisions I made, I think. I wanted to get into the theatre. I'd shown no particular sign of ability at that time, but I felt that I could do it somehow. I don't know why, really. Then I went to a technical college and learnt shorthand and typing, did a few sort of odd jobs for a short time and then when the war started I went into troop entertainment.

I started making a living at the Windmill. We did six shows a day, six days a week, and you learnt to die like a swan—you know—gracefully. I mean I used to go on—the show used to start at 12.15, I used to go on at 12.19 to three rows of gentlemen reading newspapers, and nothing, you see, absolutely nothing, but you'd learnt to die with a smile on your face and walk off. Then you came back again at two o'clock to the same people, and you died again you see. But it was a great experience. I didn't enjoy it at the time, but it's been a great benefit afterwards. The best thing was when the drunks used to come in about twenty past three, when the pubs were closed. They were quite lively—sort of made the day go. After the Windmill there were quite long gaps. There were a lot of summer seasons and things that were valuable experience to me during this time, and only a few broadcasts.

An individual performance is a bit of hell just before it starts. There's a lot of champing around and trying to get the right edge so that you are relaxed but also have a kick, so that you're going to be alive and also relaxed. It means a great deal of concentration and hold upon yourself to do this. It's a little too quick to really enjoy, I think. But there you are, it's very challenging. It is enjoyable as a whole.

I've been very fortunate, I think. I have everything that anybody could want to make them happy. The only happiness I can achieve would be to perfect the talent that I have, whatever it may be, however small it may be. That is the whole purpose of it, and that is the whole purpose of what I do.

I wouldn't expect happiness. I don't. I don't think it's possible. But I'm very fortunate to be able to work in something that I like. I think to work in something that is pleasure is all anybody can ask. If such a time came that I found that I'd come to the end of what I could develop out of my own ability, limited however it may be, then I wouldn't want to do it any more.

When I applied for the post of General Manager of the British Broadcasting Company, I literally didn't know what broadcasting was. The advertisement was attractive; I thought it seemed the sort of thing I wanted. I addressed an application to the man to whom it was said applications were to be addressed; posted it in the letter-box of the Cavendish Club in Piccadilly; then did what I ought to have done before writing the letter—looked up the man in *Who's Who*, and I retrieved my letter from the club box; rewrote the letter with a reference to my Aberdonian ancestry. And that, I think, ensured me for the short list.

I was perhaps more conscious of religion in my early home life than anything else. There were prayers morning and night. Church, every Sunday twice, and Sunday school as well. And when I got older the Wednesday evening prayer-meeting. I liked to go to all these services. I enormously admired my father's preaching; and the music was very good. I don't think I had any doubt in those early years; I certainly never expressed any doubts to him. I never had—nor yet have—doubts about fundamentals. One sat more loosely to certain points of dogma and doctrine as one got older, but as to fundamentals, no change. But I am a poor practitioner; I believe profoundly but practise poorly.

I did not become at all close to my father till I was twenty-six, and he seventy-five.

There was great love from both my father and mother, but there was an austerity in the surroundings, and I never learnt that life was for living. I don't know that that has come to me even yet. Whatever of that sort might have come—or might be coming—doesn't derive from the climate in the manse of the College Church in Glasgow.

One of the fondest pictures I have of those days is my father preaching in the pulpit of the College Church. He was six foot three and tremendously impressive; with a most beautiful voice, and a smile that was benign.

I am six foot six when I stand straight. I reached that height when I was about twenty-three, but I remember Lord Roberts asking me at Aldershot what height I was—six foot two at seventeen. I've too much strength, and have had all along, I think. I wish I weren't as tall as I am. It's awkward; anything over six foot two is an affliction.

I'm incapable of the technique—the devices and expedients—which ambition, in the ordinary sense, almost inevitably compels. I've been ambitious in this other sense—minded to do whatever came to one's hands with all one's might—both hands; to do whatever it was better than, or at least as well as, anybody else could—and in shorter time. To be fully stretched. Not ambitious for this or that position. Except in so far as this or that position would make one fully stretched, and all one's capacities and intelligence and strength be used. I was about eighteen when I first felt like that—consciously.

On the top of Ben Macdhui in the Cairngorms in Inverness-shire I realized something of my powers. I had just been climbing all day long. I'd been up Cairngorm and down to Loch A'an, and the shelter-stone, and then up one of the difficult chimneys of Ben Macdhui, and I had been wondering whatever I was going to do in the world. The prospect was

pretty bleak, because I didn't know what I wanted to do. I only felt conscious that I ought to be able to do all sorts of things, but how to set about them? Ignorant—and no help from anybody. I was just seventeen.

Nobody can talk to me today about hours or conditions of work, because I served a five-year apprenticeship in locomotive shops in Glasgow, and it was a very trying period. But it was of immense value in some ways. But whether there was more lost than gained, I wouldn't know. Five years—getting up at a quarter to five every morning, except Sundays, and working from six o'clock till five thirty, and most of the time three hours' evening classes every night.

The first decision to be taken was whether or not the British Broadcasting Company Limited should have its licence extended after its first four years. It had had a two-year licence, then a committee recommended another two years—that's four—and then I felt strongly that it should be turned into a public corporation—the first of its kind. There was opposition to that, to a considerable extent from one's best friends. The B.B.C. had been in the hands of the wireless trade, but they had never dictated policy decisions or anything of that sort. They had given me virtually full freedom of management, and allowed me to manage the B.B.C. Company in the interests of broadcasting itself and of the country. But there was a danger that another board of directors might not be as broadminded and far-seeing; I felt that it should become a public corporation, and I strongly urged that, with the permission of my own board, which was given to their great credit, I feel.

In the early days there were many fights with Government. Finance, that was the first cause of trouble. Then as to the handling of controversy. There was never any attempt to interfere with salaries. There was never any attempt to interfere with such matters as the introduction of the *Radio Times*, nor, still more controversial, the *Listener*—though there nearly was some interference there—the Prime Minister personally.

I suppose I imposed my own views; but my own views were not just the product of my own imaginings, or principles, or characteristics. There was a very large measure of devolution, and many senior executives were party to decisions taken—decisions on religious policy, for instance.

There was a Board of Governors over me, in whom *de jure* all responsibility and authority were vested. I never claimed any *de jure* authority or responsibility—never—though an enormous amount—ninety-nine per cent, maybe—was given to me, not taken, *de facto*, by the Board. They could intervene if they wanted to. They were given opportunity of expressing themselves on all major issues, and on several minor ones likely to attract attention. There was a very strong executive system. In the first three months I established what was called the Control Board—the senior executives meeting weekly; and it was unusual for decisions to be taken merely because I had said what I felt. If I were asked, 'Do you wish to have yes-men?' 'Of course I wish to have yes-men,' I might reply, but yes-men who expressed fully and freely and with any emphasis they liked their point of view, but who would then

accept mine even if quite different from theirs. Throughout—though undoubtedly I framed, formulated, and saw to the execution of various policies—by and large it was with the entire approval of the Board of Governors, which changed every now and again. And, by and large, with the approval of the senior executives.

One of the most deplorable and shocking mistakes ever made in public affairs was when the B.B.C. monopoly was broken and commercial broadcasting introduced. The public, by and large, were satisfied with the B.B.C. as it was before the monopoly was broken; anyhow as it was when I left it.

If it's said that the B.B.C. declined in competitive spirit, and energy and imagination after I left it, I should be very sorry, but I'm not in a position to deny it.

A great many changes in the B.B.C. since I left, were not inevitable, and I regret them. I believe that businesses of every sort, or almost every sort, depend on one man, whether he's Executive Chairman, or Chairman, or General Manager, or whatever; they depend on one man for success.

I know of only one case of overt interference from Government, but I know of several cases where there were endeavours to influence.

I never listen to the radio, or watch television. When I leave a thing I leave it. I was mightily interested in programmes when I was in the B.B.C.; I listened night after night; I had a weekly list of things from the Head of the Programme Division that I had to listen to. When I left the B.B.C. I ceased to be able to do anything and I didn't want to subject myself to unnecessary irritation. Maybe also I thought I had better things to do.

I left the B.B.C. and regretted it, profoundly. I left because I thought it was fully well organized, capable of taking care of any development that came, war or anything. In other words, I wasn't busy enough. Quantitatively, I think I'm more busy now than I've perhaps ever been, but not qualitatively.

In the last war I regretted very much indeed that Mr Churchill didn't give me ten times as much work and responsibility as he did. I could have carried it; and I could have helped him enormously.

It may be to one's credit if one is difficult to get on with. Should one tolerate inefficiency and slow-wittedness and all the rest of it? One of the mistakes I've made is that I haven't made enough effort to do so.

I have some sense of humour, but not as much as I wish I had.

I can be unforgiving. There are a few people whom I will never forgive, or anyhow haven't forgiven yet. I have a black-list; there are only about eight people on it, for all my long life. It isn't always the same eight. I try to persuade myself that it was more my fault than I could have realized. All right,

then the man comes off, but somebody new, maybe, goes on.

Only once have I been near to violent action. My father at the age of seventy-three had been run over by a drunken van-driver one day, and I thought he wasn't going to recover; he was very badly hurt. I went out to find the man, and I got all the information the police could give me as to where I might find him; and I told the police inspector in the College Division that, if I found the man, I wouldn't be answerable for what happened. Now, I was extremely strong, in those days, and only twenty-four, but I took an inch-and-a-half spanner in my trouser pocket to make sure. I hoped I wouldn't have to use an inch-and-a-half spanner, and even if I had, I hoped I wouldn't have killed the man; but I merely gave notice that I wouldn't be responsible for what happened. I would surely have wrought vengeance on that man if I could have found him.

I have not been happy, and I have not been successful. I have wanted to be fully stretched, and possibly the positions into which one would have been most fully stretched are political. I would like to have been Viceroy of India, and I would have liked to have been Prime Minister; but not for the sake of the jobs, or the patronage or anything of that sort. There are one or two other jobs I might like now. But not for power or patronage, or anything like that, but for the full stretching.

I have never joined a political party.

My greatest trouble has been in not tolerating slowness and inefficiency. Not going at other peoples' pace instead of at my own. Not taking an hour to do a job, instead of five minutes, because the hour was the average performance. And a very great mistake was in not realizing that life's for living; I've missed a great deal through that.

Simone Signoret

A mother is a woman who is always there when the child goes to bed, when a child gets up in the morning to go to school, and I certainly am not a mother in this sense. Sometimes I am away, and sometimes my daughter goes to bed without me—very often. I'm trying to be a mother as much as I can, but I'm certainly not the best example of being a mother.

My mother's a wonderful woman. One day I remember she bought a toothbrush in a shop and she found out, when we came back home, that the toothbrush was made in Japan—that was in 1936, I think, or 1937. And she went all the way back and gave the toothbrush back to the man and said, 'I don't want that toothbrush because it's made in Japan. And you know, with the money they make with these toothbrushes, they're going to make guns and they're going to make a war. So they are for the axe.' I was listening. I wasn't understanding anything but I was following the conversation. I was blushing because the man was saying, 'Well, it's cheaper than the French.' She said, 'Yes, it's certainly cheaper, but give me a French toothbrush.' He said, 'Oh French.' 'No,' she said, 'it's not that—' Then she very steadily and very calmly would repeat her speech about the

fact that with the toothbrush's money they would make guns, so she would buy the French toothbrush which was more expensive and be very happy for the whole day. I was very unhappy because children love their parents when they are absolutely grey, unnoticeable and lost in the crowd.

When I find myself with a German man who's more than thirty or thirty-two, I get a little—I mean I start inquiring whether I don't want it. I have to. I say where were you, what were you doing, what did you think about that and that. I feel good with the kids and the young people, because I think they were not involved in the whole thing. I think there's a common responsibility for all human beings for what is going on in your country. So, with a German, it's a little hard.

The first free part I heard about, I went and I made a test. It happened to be a prostitute, but if it had been a schoolmistress I would have tried to get it.

I've played bad women and wicked women and it doesn't pay. I mean, the people don't like you after that. They hate you and they are right, because if you do it well they just don't like you because you're hateable.

I know that I can do things I couldn't do before because I've got a reserve of emotions and sorrows and joys and love, in which I can fish. Every time something happens to me in life, it's there some place in me. When the moment happens in a picture or in a play that I need to use these kinds of sentiments, they are there and I know what I am talking about. When I was younger I didn't know.

I like the independence of the life.
I like the glamour. I like the feel
of the audience. I like the luxury.

When people stop recognizing me,
I shall start to worry.

The great luxury for me is having
a car.

I always take interviews myself and
I never give out any Press releases,
so most of what you read in the
newspapers is true, if not just slightly exaggerated. But I do enjoy classical music. Sibelius and Dvorak I
enjoy very much, Tchaikovsky I
like. My brother introduced me to
classical music—he's ten years older than myself and he's always had
a love for classical music. I just
picked it up from him.

I always try to dress for the occasion.

I've read some of Aldous Huxley's
books. My favourite book is *Catche*
in the Rye by Salinger. And I'm
going to start on Hemingway and
Steinbeck now.

Whenever I meet an interesting
person I always try to pick their
brains and find out what good
books they've read, and what good
music they've listened to lately.

I thought I was dying. I felt so
mentally sick and tired—so I went
along. The psychiatrist said I was
overworking. But this was a long
while ago.

I get nerves before I go on the stage
every time.

I started work when I was very
young. I worked for my mother
and I worked newspaper rounds
when I was twelve, and I bought
all my own clothes, so I became
independent very early on. And
my mother and father encouraged
it, as they did with my brothers and
sisters.

I'm a member of a union. I'm a
member of the A.C.T.T. You
never know when you'll need it.

I started as a messenger boy for a
film company for a little while.
There were six messenger boys.
Then I left the company and went
to another, a television company,
to be an assistant film editor. And
the rest of the boys started a skiffle
group, and they didn't have a
singer, and so they asked me if I
would come in the skiffle group and
sing. And that was the first time

went down there and we re-
~~rsed~~ and practised. The very,
first professional engagement
at a boys' club in Wandsworth.
~~nk~~ we got fifteen shillings, and
was with the skiffle group. I
a couple of months in show
~~ness~~ when I went on *Six Five
~~ial~~*. I made two records and I
some stage shows and they
all deadly failures, so I got
~~eartened~~ and went back to
~~k~~. And then about a year later
~~od~~ friend of mine, John Barry,
me up at the film studios and
he was on the new B.B.C. pro-
~~me~~ called *Drumbeat*, and they
looking for new faces on the
~~w~~, and would I go along for
~~udition~~. So he fixed an audi-
for me with the producer,
~~art~~ Morris, and I went along
Stewart gave me the show.
was when it first started.
I was in the film studios, I
~~led~~ to devote myself to making
~~eer~~ and I became passionate-
~~terested~~ in it, and I worked all
~~s~~, Saturday and Sunday. Be-
I knew it I had a small savings
~~unt~~—I think it was about
or forty pounds—and that
~~led~~ me to save the rest to put
~~posit~~ on a car. So when I got
chance to go on *Drumbeat*, I
my job for three weeks, be-
the contracts were optional
~~ee~~ weeks, three weeks, nine
~~s~~ and then another thirteen—
~~tever~~ it was. So I decided to go
f it wasn't a success, I'd made
~~ey~~ off the three shows. I could
a car—put a deposit down.
after three I got signed up for
more, so I gave up the job.
~~n~~'t feel that teenagers would
their heads if I had a Yul
~~ner~~ haircut. If I put my head
gas oven, they wouldn't do it.

ADAM FAITH

The best reason I can think of for not running for President is you have to shave twice a day. I've had to do that twice, and that's enough.

My father was a professional farmer. By this I mean to say he managed farms throughout central Illinois, and my grandfather was a newspaper proprietor. My other grandfather was a politician and a lawyer. My Stevenson ancestor was a democratic politician. My mother's family were republican newspaper publishers. My great grandfather's a man of whom I'm inordinately fond. His name was Jesse Fell and he was a Quaker, and he came to Illinois from Pennsylvania, and he came to Illinois in the early eighteen hundreds and settled down. In the course of time he became a great friend of a young lawyer practising in a near-by town—they served together in the legislature—named Lincoln. He was the first one to propose the Lincoln-Douglas debates in order to popularize Lincoln as a public figure, hoping that he might ultimately thereby achieve national reputation for him. And lo and behold he succeeded. That great grandfather of mine was also the founder of the Republican Party in Illinois, and I was the Democratic Party's candidate for President twice. My father was a democrat and my grandfather was a democratic vice-president.

My father was a very gay, lighthearted man, and a very witty man. He had very poor health. He was sort of an invalid most of his life, but very bright, very quick-witted, and, as I say, a professional farmer. He introduced the soya bean, for example, which is now one of the major crops of the United States, to Illinois back in the beginning of this century. My mother was a very cultivated woman; she was something of a scholar and a student, and much more so than my father. My father was an extrovert; she was an introvert. I suppose I was with my mother much more than I was with my father because he was a very active man, going around as long as his health permitted, round the country, round the world, indeed—very active in public affairs. My mother was very much of a stay-at-home. She was very much interested in the children, in their upbringing, in their education, in their health—I thought a little too much so. She was always putting rubbers on me and always switching me if I misbehaved and got caught out cold. And every time I'd come home with a broken nose from a fight of some kind or other, there'd be a terrible tantrum and I'd have to behave myself for a while. That happened three times. I always contrived to get in fights quicker than anybody in my neighbourhood. On the whole I lost them. That's pursued me ever since.

I used always to be afraid I was going to fail my examinations, and I would wake up in the night and worry about that, and I sometimes still do. I'm still taking those examinations, over and over again.

When I was twenty I ran away with another fellow to be a rancher in Wyoming. We went to Wyoming and we bought an option. We paid almost ten dollars for it, this student and I, on a small piece of land at the mouth of a canyon in the Big Horn

ADLAI STEVENSON

Mountains. I'd spent some five years working there on ranches as a boy in the summers as a dude wrangler, cutting alfalfa and wrangling horses. This seemed to be the logical career for me. My father came out and snatched me by the scruff of the neck and took me back and dropped me in the Harvard Law School and I never escaped.

When I was in the war I went to Italy one time. I headed the first economic mission that President Roosevelt sent to Italy after the landings at Salerno and the invasion of Sicily, to see what we could do to restore the economic well-being of the Italian people. They had suffered from twenty years of Fascism, suffered from the retreats of the German army and who were in dire misery, poverty, malnutrition and hunger, and conditions were very bad. When I was there I went once up to the Liri Valley, where the fighting was going on, north of Naples, in front of Cassino. There I read a public poll taken in the United States, in the midst of all this blood and squalor and mud and cold and rain and snow in the winter of 1943, and it said that of all the American parents who had been interrogated in this poll, sixty per cent—I think the figure was somewhat larger than that—two-thirds—said they would not want a son of theirs to go into politics or serve in public office. Now this seemed to me an incongruous and intolerable thing. Here their boys were dying in misery all about me. It was all right to fight for what you believe in but apparently it wasn't tolerable to work for it. Well, this seemed to me incongruous and I felt strongly about that, and I said by golly, when this war is over, if I have a chance to do anything about it and about our government and the continuity of what we believe in, I shall do it. This sounds very pious but . . .

I've always been myself and talked of people regardless of what their station was, what their education was, as though they were all of them citizens exercising the responsibilities of choice in a democracy, and that they were entitled to the best I had.

Lots of people have said that my touch is entirely too common, so I get a little confused. I used to joke and was lighthearted. It's a pity to take politics as though it was the beginning and end of everything.

I should like most to be remembered for having made some contribution to a higher level of political dialogue in the United States than I found when I came, at the top level; that for the most part we have abused, I think, the electorate by telling them what they want to hear, by reassuring them, by giving them good news, by telling them what we think will ensure their favourable attitude towards us—in other words, to win their votes rather than to win their minds, and I think with this we defeat our own ends, that we live in a time of testing, a time of acute struggle, a time indeed in which the democratic system must either prevail or—must survive or not. And to do this we have a great and abiding responsibility; those of us who have had the fortune, the good fortune, to suffer, if you please, in the exposed positions of public responsibility, to talk sense to people, to tell them what the facts are, to give them the alternatives and the choices, in reality and not in this imaginary and euphoric dialect that we so often use—idiom that we so often use. This, I think, is what I should like to be known for if I could, and that I had lifted the level of discourse and the quality of the language, most of all, I would like to think, in the spirit of the ideas.

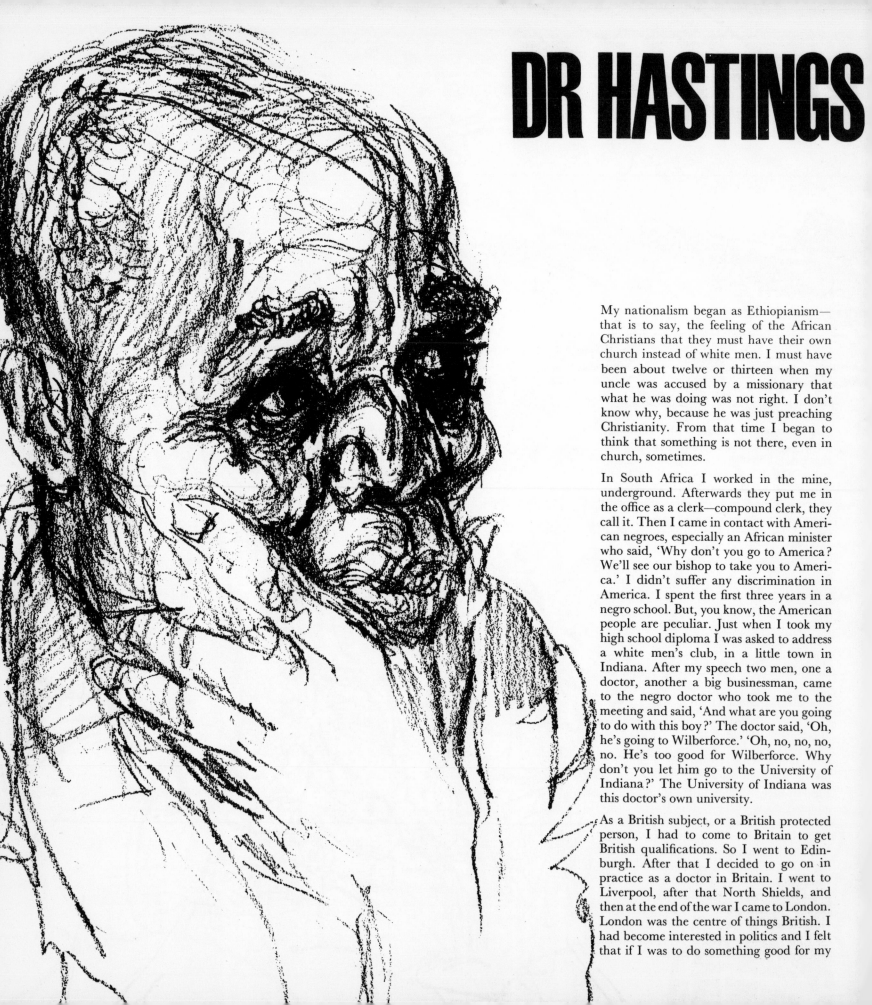

DR HASTINGS

My nationalism began as Ethiopianism—that is to say, the feeling of the African Christians that they must have their own church instead of white men. I must have been about twelve or thirteen when my uncle was accused by a missionary that what he was doing was not right. I don't know why, because he was just preaching Christianity. From that time I began to think that something is not there, even in church, sometimes.

In South Africa I worked in the mine, underground. Afterwards they put me in the office as a clerk—compound clerk, they call it. Then I came in contact with American negroes, especially an African minister who said, 'Why don't you go to America? We'll see our bishop to take you to America.' I didn't suffer any discrimination in America. I spent the first three years in a negro school. But, you know, the American people are peculiar. Just when I took my high school diploma I was asked to address a white men's club, in a little town in Indiana. After my speech two men, one a doctor, another a big businessman, came to the negro doctor who took me to the meeting and said, 'And what are you going to do with this boy?' The doctor said, 'Oh, he's going to Wilberforce.' 'Oh, no, no, no, no. He's too good for Wilberforce. Why don't you let him go to the University of Indiana?' The University of Indiana was this doctor's own university.

As a British subject, or a British protected person, I had to come to Britain to get British qualifications. So I went to Edinburgh. After that I decided to go on in practice as a doctor in Britain. I went to Liverpool, after that North Shields, and then at the end of the war I came to London. London was the centre of things British. I had become interested in politics and I felt that if I was to do something good for my

BANDA

people in Nyasaland I had to be in London at the centre of things.

I left London immediately it became evident to me that the Conservative Government was determined in imposing this scheme on us. I knew I could not keep my mouth shut in London, so I decided to go to the then Gold Coast, because I wanted to give everybody a chance—the European settlers—to prove to us that when they said that federation would bring partnership between the European settlers in Central Africa and us, they meant it. To my own people I wanted to make sure that when I led opposition to federation I was right, because I felt sure that if I was right they would stand by me and if I were not they would not stand by me.

No one is ever suited for self-government until he's self-governing.

They claim we are getting three million from the federation but what does that three million do? Into what does it go? The army, police, prison. Do you think I appreciate that? What benefit do my people get from that?

I've always argued that if you are two brothers in the mouth of the lion, and you are sensible, you must get out. You're not doing anything by remaining passive in the lion's mouth. One of you must get out and hit the lion from behind.

I feel strongly African, but of course I have adopted many of the European ways—my clothes, my language and my tastes. But at heart I'm an African nationalist. That is why those Africans who were at home are not being followed by the people now, because they did not feel as strongly as I did, and even their methods of dealing with the British Government, or the Nyasaland Government or the European settlers, has been purely that of politicians, opportunists and not truly sincere nationalists.

I was never under suspicion of having committed a war crime.

I always looked for the sort of atrocities to which hard-fighting troops are tempted to be led when they lose men by partisans, for instance. I think I achieved a different behaviour on the part of the German higher commanders, specially after we had withdrawn from the Cassino front. We were beaten and the war degenerated into a partisan war. There was not much on on the front line, but behind the lines you couldn't be safe. I had some very strange experiences there, especially near Bologna, where my own chief of staff and people wouldn't let me go alone on horseback, which I like very much as a recreation. So did my Italian friends. I had some Italian friends in Bologna. One day my Italian friend said to me, 'You go on your horse wherever you like; I talk with these people and they said, "To him we will never do any harm." ' This was just, I think, a token of gratitude for what I have done for the population there.

Before I took over the command of the 14th Panzer Corps at Cassino I was in an ambiguous position on the islands of Corsica and Sardinia. I called myself with the proud title of a *Wehrmachtbefehlshaber* but in fact I had nothing but a S.S. brigade and a division in Sardinia which I hadn't seen because I had my headquarters in Corsica. I knew I had to empty the islands when the enemy would land there as they did with French troops, much stronger than we were. Of

course it was only a question of days to capture all our soldiers or to get away. But as the armistice had been concluded the 8th—I arrived the 7th—the 8th, the Italian corps commander with whom I had to stay told me unfortunately we must separate. We must get at least twenty miles away from my headquarters because from tomorrow on we should be enemies instead of allies. Then I had the task of getting this division in Sardinia over to Corsica which is a diplomatically difficult thing because one of the islands is Italian, the other one is French, and the French had already established their regime in Corsica. But Hitler had given an order that if any Italians went on fighting after the 10th of September which was the day when he disarmed them, then they would be shot. I had to regain the port of Bastia, for instance, some days before, immediately after the thing had exploded, and therefore these officers whom I made prisoners, some hundreds of them, didn't even know anything of the Hitler conditions. And yet I was told several times to shoot them and to report their names on the same evening. Fortunately, personally, I didn't get the orders because I was on the front line. But the general staff officer got them and was absolutely out of his boots because he didn't know what to do. But the thing was resolved very simply. I got a telephonic line with Kesselring who knew me for quite a long time and said, 'This is one of the orders I shall not obey. Do what you like.' I think I must be very grateful to Kesselring with whom I didn't harmonize always. He did not take this

refusal of obedience personally, and reported it to high quarters probably with some mitigating circumstances. Immediately afterwards, when the islands were really cleared of German and Italian troops I was very highly praised even by Hitler for the achievement which he hadn't expected.

There were two dates when I thought Germany was losing. When they started it, because it was too similar to the first one, no lessons drawn from the events of the First World War. The second, when they were stuck on the 7th December at the attack on Moscow, when I was convinced that it was the turning point. Orders were given quite contrary to what the troops afterwards did. Hitler could no longer impress his will on the situation and the geographical situations of the armies there changed entirely. The third occasion was the Paulus army affair, because there you had a type of modern battle of first order strategy, not only a break through, but an encirclement which we always aimed at. This tactic offered itself because on either side of the Stalingrad army were very weak allies, very badly armed, like Hungarians, Rumanians—poor fellows who couldn't fight at all there.

I don't believe in the breaking of an oath under conditions like the German ones because we are of the opinion that the oath no longer had any value. One side was too criminal to receive an oath, although they were still looked upon as the theoretical and spiritual head of the state. It was

the sort of government which no nation ever could suffer for any length of time. So I approved of the plot against Hitler. I'm very sorry it is not celebrated sufficiently in Germany because I think it's the only movement where people really offered their lives for the sake of their nation in a direction which everybody can approve, the direction of freedom.

Hitler told us he was planning to attack in the spring of 1938. Before he started the war, he collected all the commanders down to the regimental commanders—I was regimental commander at that time. We were gathering in Berlin and the speech he made to us was a sort of confession that his endeavours to improve the German economic situation hadn't succeeded as well as it looked. The autobahn had been beautiful enough but unproductive investments, or only partly productive investments. Barracks had been built by that time. The army had been put on its feet, and yet he evidently was very much afraid of a new slump which might have cost him a good deal of popularity, of course. So therefore he said what can we do? I cannot ask other people to give up their markets, their foreign markets for myself so that they don't export anything and we the Germans make the exports. I cannot either ask them to stop flourishing economically. Therefore, the only thing I can do is to conquer more territory— as he thought this a remedy for all the economic evils which, of course, it isn't. Because when the Germans invaded Poland they saw that this country was much more densely populated agriculturally than East Prussia which was a country for big landowners.

The conscientious examination of oneself is a dialogue between your creator and yourself. The idea of having your own children suffer the same fate as the Jewish children is not a very courageous and noble motive but it is one which is humanly justifiable, I think. I was convinced—I was amazed that after the plot Hitler let so many of the wives and children of the plotters survive. They had a very bad time indeed and I confess that one of the arguments which held me back to interfere was this, that I don't think these, under the actual circumstances, neither the nation nor the people nor even much less the government was worth risking your and your family's life without the prospect of any success.

The preparation of an aggressive war can never, in my mind, be regarded as a crime by anyone. Any general staff officer, all over the world, must be prepared to make plans to clear a situation, how they may for instance conduct a defensive on a special sector and by offensive measures, which is always done. So if you are politically decided to make no other war but a defensive one, but have no military grounds to attack in order to make your defence efficient, I think it's perfectly absurd to leave it to judges, the judgment, whether the men who partook in these plannings are to be punished, maybe severely punished. I reject it. I don't think it's possible.

General von Senger

The Rev LUTHER KING

I became conscious of colour discrimination at a relatively early age. I think the first time was when I was about six years old. I had some friends whose parents had a store—two white boys, and they were my inseparable playmates for the early years of my life. I remember when I was about six something started happening. When I went over to play with them they always made excuses—they could not play, they were busy. Finally I went to my mother with this problem, and she tried to explain to me in the best way she could explain to a child six years old. And this was really the first time that I became aware of the racial differences—of the racial problem. She made it clear to me that this system had a long history, dating back to the time of slavery. She tried to explain the meaning of the system of segregation, but the thing I will always remember is that in the midst of her explanation she always said to me, 'You must never feel that you are less than anybody else. You must always feel that you are somebody, and you must feel that you are as good as anybody else.' And of course this came up with me, in spite of the fact that I still confronted the system of segregation every day.

As I look back over those early days, I did have something of an inner tension. On the one hand my mother taught me that I should feel a sense of somebodiness . . . On the other hand, I had to go out and face the system, which stared me in the face every day saying, 'You are less than', 'You are not equal to'. This was a real tension within.

In my days in Atlanta as a child there was a pretty strict system of segregation. For instance, I could not use the swimming pools. For a long, long time I could not go in swimming until the Y.M.C.A. was built, a negro Y.M.C.A. and they had a swimming pool there. Certainly a negro child in Atlanta could not go to any public park. I could not go to the so-called white schools. There were separate schools. And I attended a high school in Atlanta, which was the only high school for negroes in the city. And this was a real problem because in Atlanta there are more than two hundred thousand negroes. In many of the stores downtown, to take another example, I could not go to a lunch counter, to buy a hamburger or a cup of coffee, or something like that. I could not attend any of the theatres—only there were one or two negro theatres. They were very small. They did not get the main pictures. If they got them they were two years late, or three years late.

I remember as a child seeing problems of police brutality. This was mainly aimed at negro children, and negro adults. I remember the Klu Klux Klan.

I remember seeing the Klan beating negroes on some of the streets there in Atlanta.

When I was about eight years old I was in one of the downtown stores of Atlanta and all of a sudden someone slapped me, and the only thing I heard was somebody saying, 'You're the nigger that stepped on my foot.' And it turned out to be a white lady, and of course I didn't retaliate at any point. I finally went and told my mother what had happened and she was very upset about it. But the lady who slapped me had gone, and my mother and I left the store almost immediately.

I have been threatened many, many times. There was a time that we received as many as thirty and forty threatening calls a day, and, of course, I received numerous threatening letters. My secretary has come to the point now that she doesn't show me most of these letters but occasionally I come across them. They say such things as, 'You are causing too much trouble in this town and if you aren't out within ten days, you and your family will be killed.' In Montgomery our home was bombed twice.

In Montgomery, Alabama, we got no protection from the law enforcement agencies. In fact, one of the big problems in the South is that many of the mobs and the hoodlums are aided and abetted by some of the policemen. But I must say that this is a little different in Atlanta, Georgia. When we have received threats, when we have had crosses burned on our lawn by the Klu Klux Klan, the policemen have been very diligent in attempting to protect us. So that situations vary even in the Deep South.

I don't think anyone in a situation like this can go through it without confronting moments of real fear. But I have always had something that gave me an inner sense of assurance, and an inner sense of security. And in the final analysis, even in the moments of loneliness, something ultimately came to remind me that this struggle is basically right, because it is a thrust forward to achieve something not just for negro people, but something that will save the whole of mankind, and when I have come to see these things I always felt a sense of cosmic companionship. So that the loneliness and the fear have faded away because of a greater feeling of security, because of commitment to a moral ideal.

There have been times I have had to send my wife and family away for safety, particularly when we were in the State of Alabama. But my wife happens to be one of those very strong persons who is very concerned about this whole matter and very dedicated. And I can remember a time when I sent her away for safety and a few days later she was back home because she wanted to be there.

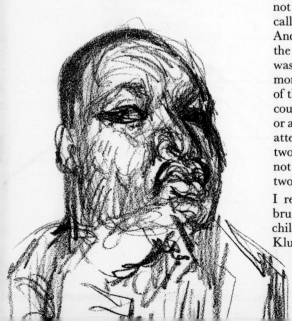

LORD HAILSHAM

I've always been surprised at the jobs I've been asked to do. I mean if anyone had told me, when I first entered Parliament, in 1938, that I would successively be First Lord of the Admiralty, Minister of Education, Chairman of the Conservative Party, Leader of the House of Lords and Minister for Science, I should have thought he was crazy.

I found it very surprising that if I had just behaved as I wanted to behave, and as I felt like behaving in the circumstances, it seemed to intrigue people enormously. Take a simple thing like bathing in the sea. I see nothing eccentric in that, but apparently it was considered extremely odd. What surprised me was that anyone bothered to photograph me doing it. I wasn't the only one in the sea at the time.

I'm in politics to do good . . .

I felt very conscious, when I was about nine or ten, after the First World War, that I was interested in public affairs. I felt I wanted to speak about them, I felt I wanted to influence people about them, and oddly enough, I had strikingly powerful, although only immature, convictions.

My father did consult me before taking a peerage—he didn't take my advice. I thought he was making a mistake from his own point of view, and I advised him not to. I was very young, of course, I was twenty-one at the time. I saw no reason why he should take my advice. I thought it was very decent of him to consult me. I think I would have resented it if he hadn't. After all, he was affecting my life, as much as his own. But I saw no obligation on him to do what I wanted. It was his life and his decision. The other day I found a letter I'd written to him at the time in which I said: 'Some people are born to peerages; some gain peerages and some have peerages thrust upon them.' That was how the letter began. He told me that he had to choose between the chance of being Prime Minister and the certainty of becoming Lord Chancellor. I said to him that I thought the right thing for him to do was to stay in the Commons. I also made it clear that I didn't want to succeed to a peerage, but I still think that I gave him disinterested and wise advice, even though I was very young.

My father always used to say, 'The one trouble about Quintin is that he doesn't suffer fools gladly.' And I dare say there was an element of truth in it. He was a pretty shrewd judge of character.

When I was a very little boy, my father came up to me at nights and explained to me, amongst other complicated things, including the structure of the atom as it was then understood, he explained to me the whole of the law of libel, so that when I actually came to do the Bar exams I knew it backwards. And he explained to me the Moneylenders' Act, too, which is very complicated. He gave me very positive moral ideas and a tremendous respect for intellectual integrity and clarity of thought. I've no doubt that I loved him, and I have every reason to believe that he loved me.

My temperament entirely is my mother's temperament. She was gay, and effervescent —frightfully good company, being bad-tempered occasionally. She was quite a different character from my father in that way. Of course, she came from America which makes it less clear, but she came from the Southern States of America and as far as I know, all her ancestors were either Scots or Northern Irish.

A good many of my so-called indiscretions are very closely premeditated. I always recognized that I was going to be a peer before I could reach what would be the serious aims of an ordinary commoner's ambition, and I'd always assumed that that would be the end of my political career. I had intended, when my father died, and I actually carried it out, to go back to the Bar, absolutely full-time, and to take silk and ultimately to go on the bench. And my political life, before that, was based on the fact that I thought it was going to end fairly soon. I was a young man in a hurry.

Like anybody who concentrates on intellectual things, I'm absent-minded. I can forget altogether about them. On the other hand, I think my work is done in a methodical way.

I say my prayers morning and night. I go to church every Sunday. I attend Communion on Feast Days. I can accept the authority of the Bible and Our Lord. I think one of the virtues of belonging to the Church of England is that you don't mind very much if you differ from the Archbishop of Canterbury.

All my life I've belonged to the Established Church in religion, to the Conservative Party in politics, I've been loyal to my family and I believe in the solid virtues of loyalty. But very often indeed I misbehave and cock a snook at authority.

I've never openly, deliberately and defiantly apostatized, but it would be fair to say that, oh, for perhaps ten years, I wasn't a believer in any sense. I didn't believe in either God or religion.

I trust God, which is the important thing.

If God exists, every human being needs to live under His authority, and the secret of happiness is to do so.

Family life is the thing I would put highest amongst my satisfactions. My first love was undoubtedly the law. Politics, however, has been, as it turned out, my deepest interest, I'm afraid.

I don't think one's family life is spoiled by politics—obviously you give up a great deal in the way of privacy. You have to take particular care about your children, who, of course, constantly see rather peculiar things about one in the Press. And I suppose they get rather teased at school. It does affect one's private life, all the time, but I don't think it's spoiled.

You don't succeed in keeping home life and official business separate, at all. I mean the red boxes come at all hours of the day and night, and so does the telephone. But you do what you can and you fight for it.

I enjoy things. I read. I climb mountains when I've got a chance. I bathe. I shoot. I enjoy shooting very much. I enjoy the countryside. I enjoy gardening enormously. I go on my farm . . . I'm interested in the farming side of it, the cows and the milk and so on.

I've tried to do all the things I've set out to do, and a good many more. In politics I've probably succeeded beyond my wildest dreams. . . . But all the other things I've rather fallen short of what I'd hoped. Climbing, for instance—I should like to have climbed the Swiss Ridge of the Matterhorn. I should like to have traversed the Grepon and so on, and I've only done a long series of rather second-rate climbs. And all the other things I've done rather less well than I would like.

I think I've succeeded beyond my wildest dreams.

QUINTIN HOGG

Sir Compton Mackenzie

I'm a jolly good sleeper. I read till about four in the morning.

This old nurse of mine must have been about fifty-five when she came to us and took me on, and she really was an early Victorian. This was very valuable for me because I learned about unreasonableness. I had to deal with an unreasonable woman. If you wanted something you couldn't have it, just because you wanted it, which is really unreasonable. You weren't allowed to have egg; you had to have water in your milk, warm water and porridge, which is absolutely disgusting. I never asked why because I came to the conclusion that it was no good asking grown-up people why things had happened. In any case she'd say, 'Why, because it is.' The answer would have been so valueless I didn't bother, I made up — I found out the answers why myself.

From three till seven was a difficult time.

I can hear it now — two hansom cabs came down Avonmore Road there, just by Hammersmith Bridge, and it was, I suppose, Easter Week — Holy Week of 1889. I was six at the time, and there arrived a man called Coward with a certain Lady Crijean saying, 'Oh, you've got to come and dine, both of you, tonight, at the Victoria' — at the Hotel Victoria. Well, now, in 1888, 1889, the only places that people dined out at were the Savoy, which had started in 1888, the Grand Hotel in Northumberland Avenue and the Victoria. Nowhere else did people dine. There was no Cecil even, certainly no Ritz, or any of these things, and you dined at the alarmingly late hour of half past seven, which was rather an extravagant time to dine. And my mother said (I can hear her now) she said, 'Oh, I don't think we can, it's the children's last night.' And Coward said, 'I'll put that right.' And my father said (I think he must have been one of my father's backers) said, 'Oh, I think we must go.' So off they went and as he went he handed me a ten-shilling piece, and as I went up to my bedroom I thought — I didn't think it in these words, but this is the emotion behind it which I still retain — you could never afford in life ever again to depend on anybody's love, you must always be prepared to be let down. And I opened the window and slung this ten-shilling piece out into the night.

I read before I was two so I was pretty precocious.

I went to a kindergarten at five, and was dressed up in an infernal Little Lord Fauntleroy costume. I thought I really can't stand this thing, and so I deliberately fell down and cut it. I cut my knees too, doing it, but I was determined not to wear a Little Lord Fauntleroy. I was a year and a half younger than anybody at St Paul's when I went there. I left the late Archbishop of Canterbury, Archbishop Temple, behind me, in the class below me. He was older —two years older.

I did much too much well at my prep school and I realized then that this must be given up, getting prizes every time, because otherwise I saw that I would be exploited—that I would be made to go into the Civil Service.

I'd made up my mind to go to Magdalen. I made up my mind to do that. My father was playing in Oxford in June, and it was the June of the Diamond Jubilee, just before it, and I went up to stay with him. I remember sitting in the hairdresser's. Then I walked round, looking at colleges, and then I went to Magdalen. 'Ah, this is for me,' I said. 'This is where I go.' And that's where I went.

I was relieved, indeed, just after Ladysmith, just after my seventeenth birthday. I was going to school, a gloomy day, a gloomy time, and I thought, I cannot walk up and down this infernal Hammersmith Road any more. I've been doing it four times a day since the year 1891, and this is now 1900, January 1900. I really must leave, how can I leave? I know what I'll do. I'll stay awake for a fortnight, and get something like a nervous breakdown. And so I did. I stayed awake for a fortnight walking up and down my bedroom reciting Keats and Swinburne and so on to myself, and Virgil. And I got a very good imitation of a nervous breakdown. So I was sent to see Dr Sidney Rayner in Upper Cavendish Place who from behind an oil lamp looked at me and said, 'What's the game?' And I realized he knew. I said, 'Well, the game is I must leave school.' He said, 'What are you going to do if you don't?' I said, 'I'll enlist in the Imperial Yeomanry.' He was sensible enough to say, 'I'll take you away.' So I went down to recover from this nervous breakdown. I went down to Bournemouth to a hydro, and in twenty-four hours I was absolutely entirely recovered.

What I wanted to do was to write plays. That's what I thought I was going to do. I'd never thought of writing novels, that was quite an accident. Then my first play was done up here in Edinburgh. I wrote my first play to appease my father for getting married when I was twenty-one, because with that lack of reason of most parents he carved my allowance the moment I got married, which was the sort of silly thing parents did in those days. And then I wrote this play to appease him and it was produced here at the Lyceum, Edinburgh, in March 1907—fifty-four years ago. Nearly fifty-five years ago. It was a great success and everything else, but the actors didn't really do —they weren't my notion of the thing, do you see. I'm too good an actor to be a good playwright, let me put it that way. You see the parts must be played exactly as I hear

them in my own head. If they aren't they don't come to life to me. So that autumn I went to live in Cornwall. My first book of poems had just come out, and I sat down one evening casually, as casually as that, to write an ideal performance of my play and that was my first novel. After that I went on writing novels. I haven't bothered about plays.

I went to the War Office and they said, 'Go away, we don't want married subalterns of thirty-one.' So I said, 'Damn it, I hold a commission, I did three years of it.' 'Oh, no, no, you go back and amuse us. Go back to Capri. Your job is to amuse us.' And then I tried to get out to Egypt but nothing doing. Then, by luck, Sir Ian Hamilton was reading *Sinister Street* on his way out, and a friend of mine in the House of Commons said to him, 'Enjoying that book?' He was, and my friend said, 'Mackenzie wants to get out.' Hamilton said, 'Oh, I'll telegraph Eddie Marsh and get him made a marine.' So I was made a marine by Eddie Marsh.

I realized that you can't go on with this elaborate prose which I'd developed in my earlier books. If you'd written ten thousand telegrams, as I had, at one and sixpenny halfpenny or something a word, you know you've got to cut out everything you really never want. Then I read Stendhal and I thought that's really the way to write, just put down what's to be said, not be bothered with decorating so much. I think that's what really happened.

I write for money. I've never saved any money. I've got to earn my living. I like living a certain standard. I like a nice house, background and everything, so I've got to earn my living.

I did a comic strip once. You see I like to know what one can do. If you're asked, do you think you could do a comic strip, well, I want to know whether I can do a comic strip. It's quite a difficult thing to do, and I've had an enormous admiration ever since for comic strippers.

I'm absolutely truthful. It's all too vivid for me to do anything else.

The earliest thing I remember is at seven months. I was seven months old. I was being taken out by a nurse, whose name was Bush. I can see her now and she left when I was a year old. I can see her now in a blue cloak with a bonnet —at Keswick, this was, holding me up, picking me out of the pram and holding me up and there was black rabbits and white rabbits roaring about in a field near Keswick. Now you see that scar. I got that in 1886. I was three— hardly three and a half—and walking beside the pram in which my brother was, with the nurse. Suddenly a gang, a chain gang of convicts appeared. I can see the warders now with trim beards and short carbines running around and yapping at them, keeping them in line and that sort of thing. And at the very end of the line there was a tall

chap about six foot three, with a very gaunt face and an expression in his eyes, of absolute despair, and on me came, and it's never gone, it's never left me since, this compassion for people who are doing this thing. And my nurse said, 'Don't turn round and stare at those poor men.' I turned quickly, and the pointed bricks of Portsmouth Barracks banged my cheek. And I can see now these drops—slow drops of blood dropping under the pram, at the side of the pram—I was taken to a chemist and patched up—but that's the scar.

All my life I've wanted people to be happier and better. I think the Welfare State has its irritations and everything else, but I rejoice that I've lived to see it. I can go back, and remember that London of the 'eighties, and by Jove, if you can remember the beggars then, and the misery—I remember being terribly upset coming to Liverpool Street—a four-wheeler—we were loaded with luggage, and a chap running behind for the sake of a bob to go up and carry all the heavy luggage. Up three flights. I can see the chap now, with a very thin shirt which had a hole and you could see his ribs—for a bob. To me really it was very painful, as a child, all this. And I always asked myself when I was very young: Why should people be poor? Why should people be poor? Why are some people made poor?

I've suffered pain—an immense amount of violent physical pain, which is very good—I'm grateful in a way I did have it when young because I think it's very valuable for anybody to have pain when he's young, in his twenties, really bad pain. I think it started probably by a couple of scrums collapsing on my leg. It didn't break my leg but it was black and green for about three months, laid up with it, in absolute agony, and then later in life it developed, I think it had some sciatic thing. It's a sciatic nerve which goes, when I'm tired, not physically tired—it's mental fatigue that gives it to me. I have this violent pain—so violent. Quite intolerable. Left Gallipoli with it, left Greece—I mean I've had it—it's always present with me. If I say, 'Yes, I will speak next April on such and such a thing,' I always say, 'but I may let you down.' It's always there. It isn't a burden in one sense because I don't allow it to be. It's a good thing—I'm a very ebullient person and I think it's a good thing that I should be laid out like this I might have been intolerable if I hadn't.

I don't think I have wasted my gifts. I've tried to entertain the world. I come from generations of entertainers and it's a natural thing for me to want to amuse people. My mother used to say, 'I think Monty will spend his whole life going round the world amusing people.' To some extent I've managed that. I wasn't prepared to put it all into Greek or Latin. That was all. I don't think I've wasted my gifts.

Lord MORRISON of LAMBETH

I don't expect Lord Attlee to admit it and he didn't admit it to me when I, in a way, raised it with him. But I think he did hang on to power—I'm afraid he did—until it was too late for me to take over from him. Why he should I don't know, because I'd given him loyal service, tried to help him in every conceivable way and relieved him of a lot of labours. But I'm afraid it's true. He hadn't had a bad run —1951, after the Labour Government was defeated, some few months after that, would have been the natural time for him to have retired.

He was a somewhat difficult man to be close to, to know exactly how his mind would be working, because he didn't reveal it too much. I can't say that he manifested any positive mistrust, but it could have been there, in view of this somewhat cold and distant relationship on the whole. I knew of some behind-the-scenes discussions that some influential Labour Members of Parliament had had with him and I was told that he intended to retire much earlier than he did. And then he didn't, so I suppose it was a matter of time, that as the years went on, I began to scratch my head and say, well, there's something funny here. Is it because I am a child of the elementary schools? It was a difficult thing to ask him about, you know, unless you appear to be fishing, or trying to push a man out and trying to push yourself in. There did appear an interview in a newspaper with him, in which he talked about looking after the young men who were coming up, whereas after all he'd hung on until he was quite a ripe age, you see, and I said what was the idea of this interview. Was it to discourage the Party putting me in? Oh no, no, no, no, no, not at all.

I thought he'd make quite a good Prime Minister, and, of course, it depends what the country wants. He wasn't a forceful leader and I don't think the British people understood him too well, but he would live at peace with the various elements in the Party and he was quite a good Prime Minister as Chairman of the Cabinet and so on. The only point I raised was that

there had been discussion after the Macdonald episode, when what is known as the betrayal took place in 1931 as to how the rights of the Party could be protected, and similar things be prevented in the future. I raised the question as to whether there ought not to be just a little delay in going to the Palace until the Party had met so that they could freely choose the leader who I had little doubt would be Attlee. As a matter of fact, the Party did meet *after* he went to the Palace, about the next morning, I think it was, and I myself moved him as Leader of the Party.

You can't snatch leaderships in the Labour Party; it's much too cautious and conservative to do that sort of thing.

I've got into more trouble by not making trouble than by making it!

Attlee was a good Prime Minister and did quite well. I wish he was a bit more hail-fellow-well-met, that's all. Then. Today. Anytime. I mean, as far as he can be.

Attlee had said that if he had been there things might have been different, which, if I may say so, I thought was a bit unkind, and not playing the game. He was kept informed in hospital of everything. He saw all the ministers in dispute, the chaps who were thinking of resignation, and Gaitskell, and myself. He was told about everything, and I have every reason to believe that he was in agreement with the course of events that took place, including the way I was handling things. For him to cast doubt upon it is not fair, it's not right.

And, of course, the dilemma that we got to in the end was that you'd either got to face the resignation of Aneurin Bevan, which was bad, or you'd got to face the resignation of Hugh Gaitskell as Chancellor of the Exchequer, which was also bad. It was a horrible dilemma, and the conclusion was reached that something's got to be decided, and it was. Resignations followed, but heaven knows, I did all I could to avoid them—and Attlee knew everything. There might have been a way that he might have

persuaded somebody to give way. I don't know. But I think he'd have had his work cut out, you see, either way. And as for compromise, we all thought about it and all considered it but it didn't come off. And after all, the issue was quite a limited one, quite a narrow one. The worry was (and it had worried Cripps before, as it worried Gaitskell) that the National Health expenditure was mounting and apparently out of control. On the other hand, Aneurin Bevan perfectly naturally was keen to develop his National Health Service and spend all the money he could get hold of.

It was a great physical problem running that Parliament with only a majority of six, and the scenes were a little bit on the disgraceful side, you know, when you come to wheeling chaps into the lobby and sitting them up in chairs. Some of them looked very bad and unpleasant and it was worrying the whips. There was a limit to how long you could go on in that situation.

My leadership would have been bound to be different from Attlee's because temperamentally I'm a different sort of man. More clearcut, more emphatic, and probably closer to the ordinary common or garden chap in the street. But otherwise, on the essentials of policy, I don't suppose there would have been a terrible lot of difference.

Attlee was a follower rather than a leader, and he wouldn't stand up against prevailing thought in the Party, even if he thought it was wrong—wouldn't stand up to it enough. On the other hand, he certainly had courage on some matters. I mean, if you take the decision on India, in which he played probably the leading part, though Cripps, Pethick-Lawrence and Alexander were backing him up and urging him on—that was courageous, and he deserves very great credit for it. Great credit.

I don't like the use of force, only I must say that I don't like this habit that certain countries are getting into, of scrapping international agreements, repudiating them and doing just what they jolly well like. You

see, we'd got a running agreement with Persia, for example, and all that happened was that the Persian Ambassador came to me and announced that they'd seized our oil installations, and I said this is too bad, you know, this is very, very serious, let's talk about it, and the only answer I got— from a very nice Ambassador—was, 'Well,' he said, 'I'm sorry, Your Excellency, but I'm not allowed to talk. I'm only allowed to tell you.' Well, that's too bad, you know. It's very naughty. I don't think the British are always wrong myself. I think quite often they're right. The foreigners are sometimes wrong. And occasionally they should be taught a lesson. As long as it's not too much trouble and as long as you've got public opinion with you.

In the War Cabinet, Winston and I got on very well normally. The only trouble was that on a certain limited number of occasions, I didn't agree with him, said so, and argued him to a standstill, and a few times, as a consequence, he didn't get his own way, which annoyed him very, very much indeed. I quite understand that, but then within forty-eight hours we were quite good friends again, and it was all right. Of course, he did go to South Lewisham on the eve of the 1945 election and he said at the bombsite there that of all his late colleagues he never wanted to see again it was me, and for about three weeks he wouldn't talk. But Winston's a kindly fellow at heart, you know. He can't go on like that for long and he made a gesture one evening at No. 10 at a party and we've been jolly good friends ever since. Of course, he's attacked me bitterly in opposition.

I think I had got something to contribute to the Labour Party. I did know the British, and I understood them and Parliament, too, and I think it might have been a good thing for the Party, and for Gaitskell, if he'd agreed to be number two until I saw fit to retire, which I would have done. However, it didn't work out that way, and therefore good luck to Mr Gaitskell. I hope he succeeds!

Lord Morrison

My dad, who was a member of the Trade Union and Labour Movement, made me open my first pay packet and join the Union with it. I thought he was a shocker. I wanted to take it home to Mum — you know the way kids do when they get the first pay packet. But Dad said to me quite clearly, 'This is the place where you get your protection — you go and join the Union.' And that was that. That was my first week in the Union.

One thing stands out in my mind particularly, as a young lorry driver in the times of the depression. I happened to be in a transport café on the Great North Road, when a young couple came in with a child in a nearly broken-down pram. They were walking from Shields — Shields was one of the places that got hit in the slump. And they were walking from there to London, because the man understood that he could get a job in London. And they came into the café and sat down, and they fetched a baby's feeding bottle out and it had water in. They fed the baby with water, and then sort of lifted the kiddy's dress up — it was a baby, a real baby — and it had a newspaper nappy on. They took this off and sort of wiped the baby's bottom with the nappy they'd taken off and then picked up another newspaper and put that on for another nappy. And I think if ever I felt a resentment against the system it was on that occasion. I thought somebody ought to do something about it. I won't say I thought I ought to do something about it. But I thought somebody ought to do something about it. We'd gone through the disputes and the strikes in '26. But here was the oppression being brought home to an innocent defenceless child and — oh, along with a lot of other lorry drivers we sort of helped them on the way. It made a profound impression on me.

One recognizes that there is power. It's good to have power if one feels wrongs should be remedied. I think with having great power one has to be careful and responsible. But it is very essential to have the power, if the wrong is going to be righted.

There's an angry man in me, all right. I'm sometimes a bad-tempered man but it doesn't hurt me because in this world you can blow your top off and still be quite responsible too, as many of our leaders have shown.

I suppose I'm a little vain — I hope not unkindly. I'm bad-tempered and sometimes bad-tempered about little things. I think some people who know me as a person would say that it's astonishing that I can keep good-tempered about major issues, try to analyse them objectively, and that I'll lose my temper about my pen running out just at the moment when I'm in the middle of writing something. But I think I've probably as many faults as most people — and not many more than most others.

It would be rubbish to take a title. After all, I've fought against the Establishment all my life, both as a young man, and now in a position as leader of the Trade Union Movement. I would resent it myself if I ever succumbed to the idea of taking a title. It doesn't interest me at all.

I have a car, yes. But my relaxations — as far as one's physically able to do it now — are gardening — I'm very fond of flowers. I like to grow flowers — I like to read a bit. But I like to grow flowers.

I talk politics everywhere. There's not much else I talk about.

My wife and I did a lot of our early hand-holding in front of political meetings. I don't mean on the platform, we were in the audience then. We stood and listened to some of the great speakers of the time together.

I like chocolates. I like to be outdoors. I like to swim. I like children very much. They're perfectly honest and there aren't many people that one can say that about.

I'd like to see a better world. A better world to me means a world that's free from the fear of war. The fear of want is of course a very vital thing but this is one of the reasons why I'm so actively associated with the idea of preventing war happening again to us. One of the great tragedies of war is that the dead don't come back to us.

I want a new order of things. I don't want capitalism to have control of the right to work or the right to eat or the right to live or the right to have a place to go to. I don't want that at all.

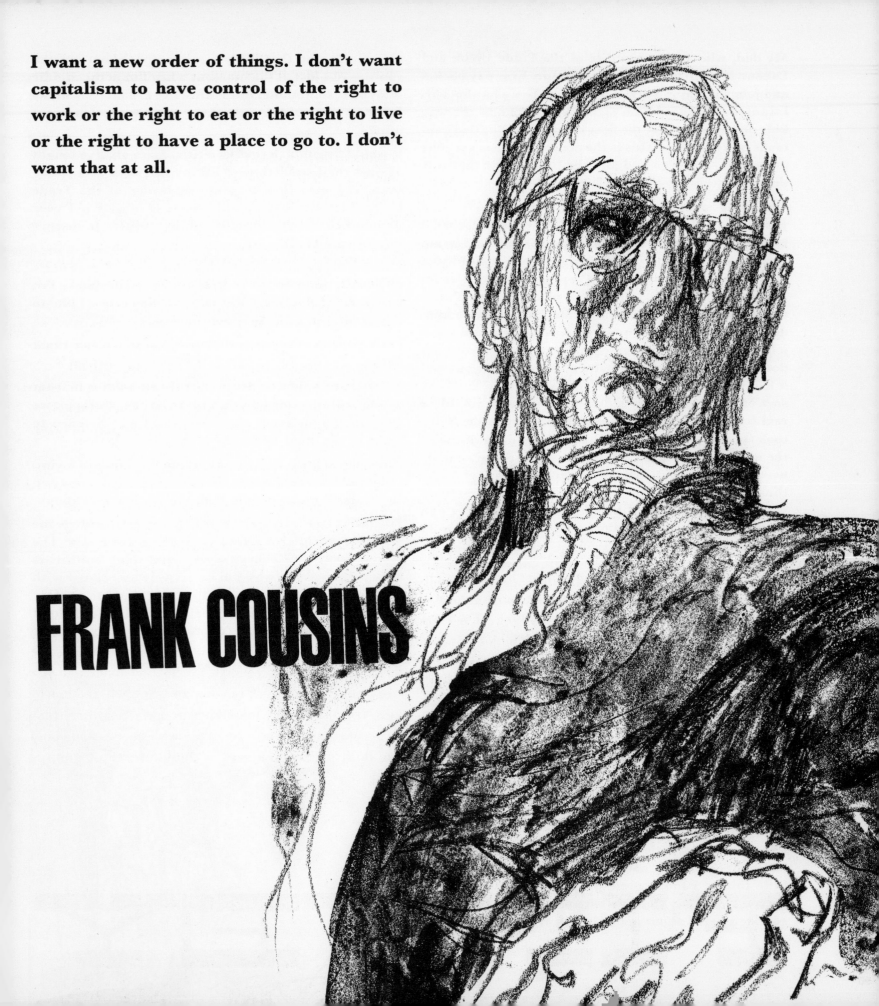

FRANK COUSINS

I went to primary school, then I went to Salford Grammar School. I entered Salford Grammar School at the sort of high stream, on the high intelligence level, but for some reason, I regarded the homework at the age of eleven rather as an imposition, and in the first term I never did any. So after one term in the high stream I was put into the bottom stream, and there I remained for about four years. I tried all the excuses of not doing homework. And then in the fourth term for some reason I suddenly worked again, and I was put up back in the high stream. That burst of intellectual activity lasted for two terms, then I faded rather, and didn't work very hard after that.

I once ran away from home—I don't know if my father knows this to this day—I ran away from home because I hadn't done any maths homework, and I didn't want to go in the next day and tell the teacher because I knew this was it. I got to the station and there was no train going where I wanted to go—I was eleven—I was going to live on a mountain in Wales, which the family called Fish Mountain where we'd been for a holiday. And I discovered that no trains went from Salford Station to Prestatyn or Rhyl, so I went back home and climbed in again through the lavatory window.

I've never really wanted to play Romeo. I've played him on a record, but I've never wanted to act him on a stage. I always feel, for instance, that when he has to get out of the bedroom, the morning when he's rushing off to Mantua, I always feel he should take her with him. He should have taken Juliet with him. Then the play would end there; there would have been no play left. I always feel the end of the play is rather pointless; she should have gone with him.

When I'm in an audience and I'm watching an actor, I can be moved by an actor, but I'm also watching him.

I'm watching—I count—I can count while he does something to see how his technique is working, but that's his. I've got to find out mine, the way I work. This is where one needs more practice when one acts. All the time one is finding out how your body works—you know—it's all right for him to do it that way, but you've got to find your way, and you can learn by watching other people act. But finally it's the amount of acting, or practice, if you like, that you do within your own body, I think.

The danger is when you become successful you get a bit of money, you go round in a large car and you can live very expensively, and then eventually all the sort of people you see are sort of very servile waiters and very expensively dressed diners. You never see people. Now I'm acting—people—it's my job, my life and I've got to see them. So in a certain sense when I leave the theatre, I just want to go out into the night, and be alone. Then I surely am able to watch people, feel that I can. This is very important to me.

I've been in love now, I think, about four times. The first time was when I was fifteen. Four times in ten years. Is that too much? I don't know. It's been rather good.

In one's own head there's a loneliness, you know. You're not lonely for people or for company, but there's a loneliness because of what is life, of one's thoughts, of one's—what I want to do in the theatre, or what one feels one wants to act, one can only communicate it really by doing it, by acting it. So in one's own head these feelings, these feelings of creation, if you like, are floating about, and you can't put them to work in company. So there is a loneliness, because there's something in one's head one can't share in company, in a room, or with people. One only can do it perhaps one day in the future, through one's work. . . .

FINNEY

EVELYN
WAUGH

'Why did you agree to appear
on "Face to Face"?'

'Poverty. We've both been hired to talk
in this deliriously happy way.'

John Osborne

My father was an invalid for most of his life. He had asthma as a boy and then he had T.B. and he always seemed to me to be in the control of other people. I remember he used to take me round to see his mother, for example, and she was a very nice woman; I was very fond of her. They were, like all impoverished middle-class people, obsessed with money and she used to taunt him with a story about how, when he was sixteen, he'd won some newspaper competition and the prize was a trip to South Africa and he'd won this prize, this competition, and on the way there he'd become ill and had to be put ashore in Lisbon, and there was a tremendous bill because of this, which they had to pay —about a hundred pounds or something. And even when he was, I don't know, thirty-four or thirty-five, my grandmother used to bring this up as something that he should still be ashamed of, and that he still owed her. But in other ways she was a very kind, nice woman. . . .

I regret my schooldays because there was a great deal of acrimony and bitterness in them. I was at this boarding school for some time, and when I was there I was unhappy most of the time. There's very little of my childhood that I can look back on with any pleasure. Most of it I regret, I think.

I'm always preparing for financial disaster, and always expecting that I'm going to end up in the bankruptcy court or prison, or nobody's going to give me a job. I think, well, who would give me a job, where could I earn twenty pounds? I'm sure I'll never really get used to having money. If I sit in a taxi-cab, I'm always surprised that I've got the fare for it.

I think the Press select their victims. Their piece of real, craven Fleet Street cant always is, of course, that if one is in the public eye, then the public has a right to know something about you. Well, this is based on the simple-minded assumption that a newspaper can reveal the truth about a human personality. It can't, of course. It's an impossibility. And what is so wicked about it is that it comes out of complete moral disengagement.